INCLUSION
in
Physical Education

Fitness, motor, and social skills for students of all abilities

PATTIE ROUSE, EdS

Human Kinetics

Library of Congress Cataloging-in-Publication Data

Rouse, Pattie, 1960-
    Inclusion in physical education / Pattie Rouse.
        p. cm.
    Includes bibliographical references.
    ISBN-13: 978-0-7360-7485-8 (soft cover)
    ISBN-10: 0-7360-7485-6 (soft cover)
    1. Physical education for children with disabilities--United States.   2. Physical
education for people with disabilities--United States.   3. Inclusive education--United
States.   I. Title.
    GV445.R69 2010
    371.9'04486--dc22
                                                        2009015391

ISBN-10: 0-7360-7485-6 (print)   e-ISBN-10: 0-7360-8750-8 (Adobe PDF)
ISBN-13: 978-0-7360-7485-8 (print)   e-ISBN-13: 978-0-7360-8750-6 (Adobe PDF)

Copyright © 2009 by Pattie Rouse

The Web addresses cited in this text were current as of June 2009, unless otherwise noted.

Essay on p. vi reprinted with permission of Delana and Elizabeth Crook.

Acquisitions Editor: Scott Wikgren; **Developmental Editor:** Jacqueline Eaton Blakley; **Assistant Editors:** Rachel Brito and Anne Rumery; **Copyeditor:** Joyce Sexton; **Graphic Designer:** Bob Reuther; **Graphic Artist:** Kathleen Boudreau-Fuoss; **Cover Designer:** Keith Blomberg; **Photographer (cover and interior):** Pattie Rouse; **Visual Production Assistant:** Joyce Brumfield; **Photo Production Manager:** Jason Allen; **Art Manager:** Kelly Hendren; **Associate Art Manager:** Alan L. Wilborn; **Illustrator:** Tammy Page; **Printer:** Versa Press

Printed in the United States of America   10 9 8 7 6 5 4 3 2 1

The paper in this book is certified under a sustainable forestry program.

Human Kinetics
Web site: www.HumanKinetics.com

United States: Human Kinetics
P.O. Box 5076, Champaign, IL 61825-5076
800-747-4457
e-mail: humank@hkusa.com

Canada: Human Kinetics
475 Devonshire Road Unit 100,
Windsor, ON N8Y 2L5
800-465-7301 (in Canada only)
e-mail: info@hkcanada.com

Europe: Human Kinetics
107 Bradford Road, Stanningley,
Leeds LS28 6AT, United Kingdom
+44 (0) 113 255 5665
e-mail: hk@hkeurope.com

Australia: Human Kinetics
57A Price Avenue, Lower Mitcham,
South Australia 5062
08 8372 0999
e-mail: info@hkaustralia.com

New Zealand: Human Kinetics
Division of Sports Distributors NZ Ltd.
P.O. Box 300 226 Albany, North Shore City, Auckland
0064 9 448 1207
e-mail: info@humankinetics.co.nz

INCLUSION

~ in ~

Physical Education

THIS BOOK IS DEDICATED
TO ALL THE GREAT PHYSICAL EDUCATORS
WHO TAKE THE TIME EACH DAY
TO ENCOURAGE AND SUPPORT ALL STUDENTS
IN THEIR CLASSROOMS.
THANKS FOR PROMOTING ACCEPTANCE
FOR STUDENTS OF ALL ABILITIES.

Delana, a third grader, wrote this essay for the National Reflections Program in her school. The theme was "How to Make a Difference." She won first place in her school and in the district.

One Saturday morning, I went to my little brother's football game and I met a special boy, named Anderson. We became friends right away. Anderson is a little different than me because he has something called Down Syndrome, and that's what makes him special.

I play with Anderson at football practice and football games. Anderson brings books and I read them to him. I also take him to the park at J.J. Biello. When he is hungry, I walk him to the concession stand. I also take him to the restroom with his brother. I want Anderson to feel like he can do what we can do. When I do things with him, I think it makes him feel good inside. I know it makes me feel good to be his friend.

Last Saturday morning, I was playing with Anderson and these kids were calling him names. So, I stood-up to them and asked them to stop. Anderson is very kind, he is funny, and he is very smart. They would know that if they gave him a chance.

I also see Anderson at school. I wave to him and he waves and says hello. He smiles and I think our friendship makes him happy.

Anderson makes a difference in my life and some day he will make a difference in yours.

When you help someone, you know you're doing the right thing.

CONTENTS

PREFACE

Inclusion in Physical Education is a book of practical strategies for including students with disabilities in general physical education. It started out as a notebook of handouts that I shared with general physical educators needing assistance including students with special needs in their general classes. The educators were very receptive to the handouts and expressed a need for a more comprehensive collection for all exceptionalities. Hence, the seed for this book was planted.

The book focuses on skill development, social development, and fitness for all students with disabilities. The suggested adaptations in this book correlate with many objectives found in the standards for physical education for many school systems, and can be implemented by any educator. Full of teaching strategies and activities for student involvement, this book gives the reader a clear understanding of how to set realistic goals for students with disabilities, which are important because they need to learn and improve skills just as their typical peers do.

In order for inclusion to be successful, educators need to consider the type and severity of the disability, the type of activity, equipment modifications, and the need for extra staff or peer support. Each chapter is filled with activities for skill development and social interaction as well as suggestions for appropriate peer or staff support. The strategies are also appropriate for students in the general class with coordination problems or with developmental delays not considered "disabilities."

This book is not based on theories or skills that can be used only by a few specially trained people. It was written on the basis of hands-on experience, trial and error, and feedback from students with disabilities. Personal experience has shown me that using simple, fundamental modifications, any educator can include students with disabilities in general physical education. I have personally used all the suggested techniques and strategies in this book with much success.

In my experience as a consultant, I have come to realize that the majority of physical educators have limited training in working with students who have disabilities. However, I have found that when given basic instruction in inclusive ideas, these teachers are extremely receptive to the idea of inclusion and become very creative in incorporating modifications for their students. For example, just making teachers aware that students can use shorter rackets for striking, or balloons or beach balls for volleying, can make a difference not only for students with disabilities but also for the general education students.

The book is divided into chapters on specific disabilities. I firmly believe that every child is a unique learner but that there are attributes that students with certain disabilities have in common. Therefore, when looking for ideas for any student with a specific disability, the reader will also gain information about other basic characteristics or expected behaviors. As the book is a quick reference for ideas for inclusion, the reader can open it and find strategies immediately.

Chapter 1, "What Is Inclusion?," supports the importance of inclusion both for students with exceptionalities and for students in the general classroom. In addition, the chapter discusses the valuable roles that paraeducators and peer facilitators play in the process of inclusion. Suggestions are given for promoting these roles and for building positive relationships with the educators as well as the students. Successful inclusion truly is a team effort.

Chapter 2, "Including Students With Autism Spectrum Disorder," provides crucial information for anyone needing assistance working with these students. The techniques for keeping students on task and part of the group, as well as the techniques for communication, are critical for any professional or parent working with students who have autism. These techniques are tried and true and can make a difference for all involved with a student with autism.

Chapter 3, "Including Students Who Use Wheelchairs," provides an abundant amount of information that I have used in my classes and as a consulting adapted physical educator. Experience has shown me that an easy way of choosing activities for including students in wheelchairs is to do so on the basis of upper body strength. Accordingly, this chapter provides many activities for the student with upper body strength or control and also for the student with limited or no upper body strength or control. It also goes a step further in providing inclusive ideas for the student with limited or no upper body strength and control who either drives an electric chair or is pushed in a manual chair. The chapter also presents various parallel activities for all of these students. Because peer facilitators and paraeducators are so important in the inclusive process for students in wheelchairs, suggestions are made throughout the chapter for their involvement. This chapter also covers modifications for a variety of sports, as well as a majority of the elementary activities used in most general physical education classes.

Chapter 4, "Including Students With Intellectual Disabilities," provides suggestions for working with three levels of students with cognitive delays; mild, moderate, and severe/profound. Expectations for these groups can be varied or the same. Characteristics of each group are discussed, and suggestions are made for inclusion and behavioral issues. Activities are also included for teaching these same students in a self-contained situation if this is the *least restrictive environment.* During my travels I have found that a common concern among other adapted physical educators is what to do with students who have severe/profound intellectual disabilities. The chapter addresses this issue by including some activities for this group of learners.

Chapter 5, "Including Students With Cerebral Palsy," discusses some of the common types of impairments with cerebral palsy and provides modifications for these students. In my experience, this group of students has proven to be one of the easiest groups to include and also one of the most rewarding groups of students to work with in a physical education setting because they have an incredible desire to succeed.

Chapter 6, "Including Students With Visual and Hearing Impairments," has pertinent information that physical educators should be aware of and should discuss with the student or with the student's classroom teacher. Modifications are included for most sports as well as games and activities used in elementary or middle schools. The chapter presents parallel activities for the student to do on the sidelines when inclusion is not possible either for safety reasons or because the activity is too difficult for the given student. The chapter also includes modifications and suggestions for students who are deaf or hard of hearing.

Chapter 7, "Differentiation in Inclusive Physical Education," correlates differentiation and inclusion. Sample drills and activities are presented that enable any educator to include students with disabilities in general physical education through differentiated instruction. In addition, modifications and adaptations are presented for varying levels of learners.

The final chapter, "Walk in Their Shoes: Games for Understanding," presents adapted games and activities that educators can use to teach general students empathy for students with disabilities. The games in this chapter can be taught in small or large groups and can give the participants insight into the lives of students with varying exceptionalities. The games provide opportunities for all students to be equal, understanding, and more receptive toward others' differences.

Any physical education teacher, paraprofessional, recreation therapist, camp counselor, church youth counselor, or parent can pick this book up and easily find instructions for including students with disabilities or delayed motor skills. The book is user friendly and provides teaching strategies that do not require extended setup time, extra equipment, or extended planning time. Professionals can find inclusive ideas within minutes of their students' arrival, which will reduce the students' anxiety and will help the teacher maintain confidence as well as fulfill curriculum goals and objectives for the total program.

As a consultant, I have collaborated with teachers who naturally include all students, those who are resistant to inclusion, and those who operate out of the fear of not knowing what to do. Using this book will provide the opportunity for the natural teacher to become more creative, for someone who is resistant to become more open-minded as a result of witnessing student success, and for someone who is fearful to gain confidence upon seeing how simple inclusion can be. I am confident that this book will make a positive difference for those wishing to include students with disabilities in general physical education. After all, these kids deserve a chance to be included.

ACKNOWLEDGMENTS

I want to thank the Cherokee County School District for embracing inclusion and providing opportunities for all children to learn. Under the guidance of the special education department, trained teachers and paraeducators who teach students with special needs become part of a community of parents, teachers, and volunteers who work collectively to improve all students' lives. I feel fortunate to have the opportunity to do what I do each day as an adapted physical educator.

A special thanks to Natalie Deviez, Gayle Allen, Ann Leverette, Denise Palmer, Lisa Swantek, Sharon Jones, Kay Relihan, Dr. Georgann Toop, Betty Harris, Shona Roberts, and Cheryl Mills. These extraordinary professionals contributed to the development of this book by answering questions, previewing chapters, and having a positive impact on my philosophy of teaching. Their contributions helped me appreciate and confirm how, as teachers and advocates for inclusion, we are stronger and more effective when we collaborate and work together toward a common goal.

Also, thanks to my developmental editor, Jackie Blakley, for helping me see and convey my vision more clearly. She and her team made the process of writing this book a challenging, yet fun, experience.

WHAT IS
INCLUSION?

Inclusion is fast becoming a daily responsibility for physical educators. For a few, this term elicits feelings of added stress and interrupts their everyday way of teaching, and for others it represents a challenge that makes them better teachers. The reality is that physical education has the potential to be one of the most supportive and active pieces in the inclusion process in schools. All children, and especially those with disabilities, learn to communicate and interact with others and develop cognitive and motor skills in physical education.

As an adapted physical educator, I have traveled to many schools and encountered many attitudes regarding inclusion. For the most part, I have come to realize that the less embracing attitudes arise from the fact that the general physical educators do not feel knowledgeable in the area of including students with disabilities in the general population. For many of these educators, little if any collaboration time is provided with special education specialists. In addition, especially in the elementary and middle schools, the class sizes are large and the physical educators feel overwhelmed about adding more responsibility to their daily routine. This book will address these issues and help physical educators become familiar with the process of inclusion. Readers will understand the importance of developing rapport and relationships with students who have disabilities, as well as with the teachers and paraeducators who support them. Furthermore, the strategies in this book will equip teachers with tools that will enable them to include all students with or without disabilities.

DEFINING INCLUSION

Inclusion refers to the process of educating students with disabilities along with their general peers. The Individuals with Disabilities Education Improvement Act (IDEIA), the United States' special education law, states that physical education is a required service for children and youth between the ages of 3 and 21 who qualify for special education services because of a specific disability or developmental delay (Boyles & Contadino, 1998). These students are entitled to a *free appropriate education* (FAPE) that is the same educational experience as that provided to their nondisabled peers. The general goal is to allow children with disabilities to be educated with their peers in the regular classroom to the maximum extent appropriate for learning, the *least restrictive environment* (LRE) (U.S. Department of Education, 2006). In other words, wherever possible, special needs students should be placed in the general classroom. For some students, this means inclusion in a classroom all day with typical peers; for others it may mean mainstreaming or spending part of the day with normally developing children. Or, some students may attend only lunch, recess, art, music, or physical education with general peers.

In many school systems, inclusion in general physical education is the first strategy used for providing inclusion to students with disabilities. The general physical educators, though not always comfortable with it, are responsible for instituting this process and are experiencing the need for support in the endeavor. In order to be effective, these educators need to be strong advocates for physical activity for all learners, need to embrace human diversity, and need to appreciate individual variations in growth and development.

There is no set way of including all students with disabilities. Inclusion is a process that is dependent upon each individual's needs. These needs are determined by an Individual Education Plan (IEP) team, which may include administrators, a special education specialist, general educators, a related specialist, and, of course, parents. The IEP can include goals and objectives for general physical education, adapted physical education, or recreation and leisure activities. For students at the high school level, adapted physical education consultation services can be sought in developing a post-school transition plan. Often the special education teacher or paraeducator records the progression of these goals and objectives. In some situations, the physical education teacher who is including the student in general physical education is responsible for recording progression. My suggestion, based on past experience, is for that educator to become part of the IEP team by attending the annual IEP meeting for the given student. Then the physical educator can provide valuable input while assisting in writing the goals and objectives.

The special education teacher will be able to provide the date, time, and meeting site for the IEP meeting. I recommend *Strategies for Inclusion* by Lauren Lieberman as a guide for working with the IEP team. Lieberman's book presents details of the steps involved in the process.

EMBRACING INCLUSION

An inclusive physical education setting can provide many positive benefits for students with and without disabilities. For the students with disabilities, physical education provides the opportunity to socialize with general peers and develop relationships, as well as to develop fundamental motor skills. Many students with disabilities do not have the opportunity to socialize outside of the school setting or participate in physical activity, and depend on this interaction to meet social needs.

For those fortunate enough to have access to outside programs, these skills help students with disabilities transition from a school to a community setting, which can have lifelong effects.

Furthermore, researchers have found that students without disabilities who experienced inclusive settings felt that the experience was valuable and taught them to deal with problems that occurred in their lives (Lieberman, James, & Ludwa, 2004). These students reported an increase in their self-worth and felt that they became more tolerant of others. They also felt that they became more understanding of others in general. Daily contact enables the general students to see the children with disabilities as "more fun" and as "more interesting" (Sherrill, Heikinaro-Johansson, & Slininger, 1994). All involved become more accepting, tolerant, caring, and giving and in turn feel more self-confident. They learn core ethical values such as respect and fairness. Fundamentally, the general students learn to become advocates for students with disabilities and in turn build character and deepen leadership skills.

To truly be included is what all children with or without disabilities want, need, and deserve; and this really is a basic human right. As educators, it is imperative that we understand this and embrace a positive attitude regarding inclusion. Any physical educator's attitude toward inclusion can determine the success or failure of the inclusive environment. I have noticed that often the general students in the classroom respond to inclusion according to how the teacher responds. If the teacher is open and accepting, the general students will be willing to work with the students with disabilities. If the teacher is not receptive, the students will not be comfortable and giving.

As noted previously, in order for inclusion to become effective, physical educators must believe in the value of physical activity for every student regardless of ability level. They must be patient with students who learn at a slower rate, and need to accept the responsibility of incorporating activities that motivate all learners with or without disabilities. They must believe that all learners can develop motor skills, feel successful, and enjoy physical activity. These teachers must use strategies to promote mutual respect, support, safety, and cooperative participation for all learners. In addition, physical educators must deliver developmentally appropriate instruction that is sensitive to multiple needs, learning styles, and experiences of all learners. An educator who sees each situation as a learning experience will enjoy the inclusive process.

It is imperative for physical educators to see the students with disabilities as children first and then to recognize the disability. For

▶ Physical activity is valuable for students of all ability levels.

example, the student in a wheelchair is not a wheelchair kid; the student with autism is not an autistic child. These students are students first and foremost, and the disability is secondary. This concept gives rise to "person-first" terminology, which educators should use when communicating with others about the student with a disability.

My experience has shown me that awareness and knowledge are key to developing positive and embracing attitudes that support inclusion. My objective in this book is to provide the basic strategies and modifications that will enable all physical educators to include students of all abilities. The activities and strategies are designed for student development and learning, as well as self-expression. Most importantly, implementing the activities will promote the importance of peer relationships for a safe learning environment.

SUPPORT FOR INCLUSION

Providing for the needs of students with disabilities and devising accommodations are a team effort, and two of the most important and available hands-on members of this team in general physical education are paraeducators and peer facilitators. Both are crucial to the success of inclusion.

PARAEDUCATORS

Paraeducators, also known as *paraprofessionals* or *teacher assistants,* generally, but not always, work one-on-one with students with disabilities. The paraeducator supports and assists the student throughout the school day in academics, art, music, physical education, recess, lunch, and toileting. Therefore, the paraeducator has great insight into the student's abilities, attitude, and desires that he or she can share with the general physical educator. The paraeducator can greatly influence the student's cognitive, social, and physical development.

Relative to physical education, the first job of the paraeducator is to transition the student with a disability to the physical education facility. The paraeducator then stays to assist the student in the planned activities, depending on the physical educator to supply any necessary equipment for modifications. In situations in which the paraeducator can give the student with disabilities space to work without assistance, he or she can assist other students in the class. It may be necessary to convey this to paraeducators so that they do not feel that they are intruding or stepping on toes if they help in this way. As we all know, it is important to communicate the needs and expectations related to the classroom environment, and most people appreciate and work more effectively knowing these expectations.

Many paraeducators have been trained to assist and interact with the student that they are working with, but experience has shown me that not all paraeducators are trained in assisting students in physical education. Therefore, the general physical educator may need to provide instructions as to what duties are expected of the paraeducators. Nonetheless, many paraeducators are experts at including their students with disabilities and are great advocates for these students' inclusion.

The following are some suggestions to provide for the paraeducator who has not been trained to assist in physical education:

- The paraeducator can relay the IEP goals and objectives to the general physical educator, as well as help implement these goals and objectives and monitor the task analysis for short-term goals.
- Paraeducators should understand that they are the student's *support* and sometimes they are essential to the the student's *success.* For example, some students may need only prompting while others may need full hand-over-hand techniques for every activity. Or, during skill development activities such as striking, the paraeducator's toss is often more important than the strike. The paraeducator must watch the student's strike and toss the ball in the zone that the student strikes.

- The paraeducator monitors the use of assistive devices for mobility and communication.
- The paraeducator is the main advocate for the student and models respect and value for that student. In circumstances of intimidation or embarrassment, the paraeducator defuses the situation in a caring and respectful manner.
- The paraeducator assists only as needed by the student. For some students this may mean use of the hand-over-hand technique, with the paraeducator actually helping the student hold an instrument or move an appropriate body part; for others it may mean simply observing until assistance is needed. In addition, assistance may include transferring a student from a wheelchair to a walker or onto a mat for an activity.
- The paraeducator can provide verbal or physical prompts for the student when necessary and senses when to move away and encourage independence.
- The paraeducator shares the responsibility with the general physical educator of providing appropriate positive feedback to the student with a disability and providing corrective feedback as needed.
- The paraeducator can encourage general students to interact with the student who has disabilities and actually assist them in partnering with the student with a disability. Facilitating social interaction is an important role for the paraeducator.
- The paraeducator also encourages the student with a disability to speak for him- or herself and encourages the student to communicate directly to the person to whom he or she is speaking.
- The paraeducator provides the reinforcements for the student's Behavioral Intervention Plan (BIP), if necessary, for the student with behavioral issues.
- The paraeducator works independently with a student in those rare cases in which the student needs to be separated from the group because of behavioral or safety issues.
- The paraeducator needs to learn the daily class routines, as well as games and activities that the physical educators teach, in order to better assist the students.

Most often the paraeducator is the liaison between the student's special education teacher and the general physical education teacher and conveys crucial information. Because the paraeducator often shadows the student with a disability throughout the day, the paraeducator is aware of limitations, safety issues, and contraindicators that will greatly influence the inclusion process. The following are some of the most common issues that paraeducators will be prepared to address when students with developmental or physical disabilities are being included.

Medical History

- A student who has a shunt needs to avoid blows to the head such as thrown balls or other objects, and the student should avoid any tumbling stunts that involve weight bearing on the neck and shoulder area.
- A student who is allergic to latex needs to avoid balloons, latex gloves, and any other type of equipment with latex.
- If a student is allergic to bees, the paraeducator needs to make sure the student always has the EpiPen when outside.
- A student who has a congenital heart defect that will interfere with cardiovascular exercise will need modifications and will need to be closely monitored.
- If a student has asthma and problems with breathing while exercising, the paraeducator knows the protocol to apply, as well as how to use the inhaler.
- If a student with visual impairments has retinal detachment, the paraeducator knows the student's limitations, which may dictate no contact to the head; no jumping, bouncing, or tumbling activities; or no running.
- If a student is prone to having seizures, the paraeducator knows the protocol for handling the situation, for example, how long is too long for a seizure to last and whether or not a parent or 911 should be called. Some students also require VNS (vagus nerve therapy or stimulation) and have a procedure to follow. In this case, the paraeducator will have training for the procedure.
- If the student has a seizure disorder, the paraeducator knows the contraindicators related to the seizures. For example, some seizures are heat induced, and the student may need to avoid strenuous exercise in a warm environment.
- If a student has a gastrointestinal tube or tracheotomy, the paraeducator knows the limitations, which may dictate avoiding trunk activities and not allowing balls to be thrown at the student.

Behavioral Issues

- The paraeducator knows the positive reinforcers for the student. Does the student need a high five, an object to hold, or positive verbal feedback?

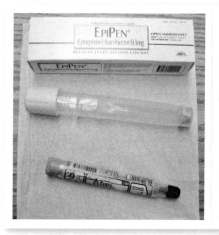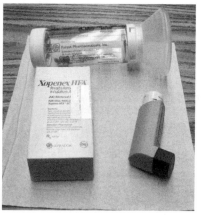

▶ An EpiPen and an inhaler.

- The paraeducator will be aware of and know how to manage the BIP for the student.
- The paraeducator will know how to de-escalate behaviors and will be aware of the "triggers" that cause the student to exhibit certain behaviors.
- Often the paraeducator is able to anticipate a behavior problem before it becomes too serious, causing the student to overreact.
- If the student has had a rough start to the day or if something happened during transition, the paraeducator will know that the student may need time to regroup.
- If the student touches others inappropriately, the paraeducator knows to monitor the behavior and provide additional boundaries.

Sensory Issues

- Does the student avoid touch or overreact to touch? Does the student need a weighted vest?
- If the student avoids close proximity to others, the paraeducator will determine if large groups are overpowering such that the student needs to work in a smaller group or one-on-one with a partner.
- Are the lights too bright for the student with autism? Does the humming of the lights lead to overstimulation?
- Does the noise level in the gym cause overstimulation followed by aggression for the student with autism?

- The paraeducator knows approximately how long the student can sit to listen to directions. Maybe the student needs to walk around the gym during this time, or maybe he or she needs to arrive after directions have been given.
- When is it appropriate for the student with autism to rock or hum in order to self-regulate?

Communication Skills

- Is the student verbal or nonverbal, and, if verbal, to what degree?
- Does the student use a communication device or sign language?
- Does the student with autism respond to lists, social stories, or picture boards?

Cognitive Abilities

- If the student is intellectually disabled, how much does he or she understand, and is he or she capable of understanding simple directions?
- Does the student need individual visual or verbal directions?

Physical Limitations

- Does the student use an assistive mobility device such as a wheelchair, walker, or cane?
- Does the student with cerebral palsy have hypertonic (tight) or hypotonic (lax or loose) muscle tone? Are stretching or resistance exercises appropriate for the student? Does the student have limited range of motion? Should the student avoid jerky movement? The physical therapist in the school can give recommendations if needed.
- How much if any vision does the student with visual impairments have? Can the student see colors or shadows or only darkness? What is the student's functional vision distance, for example, 5 inches (13 centimeters) or 10 feet (3 meters)?
- What are the limitations for the student with cystic fibrosis? Is the student allowed to participate in running, jumping, or tumbling exercises? Can the student drink regular water, or does he or she need a premixed water solution?
- Can the student with osteogenesis imperfecta (brittle bones) be allowed to participate in group activities, or should he or she perform only parallel activities on a mat?
- Does the student with Down syndrome have poor muscle tone, underdeveloped respiratory or cardiovascular systems,

or poor vision or poor balance? Does the student have a hearing impairment?

- Does the student with muscular dystrophy have a heart or breathing problem? How far has the condition progressed? Should the student be allowed to run? Is it safe for peers to assist the student?

As you can see, the paraeducator is crucial in the inclusion process for students with disabilities. Paraeducators have valuable knowledge specific to their students' needs. They know the contraindicators or activities that the student should avoid. For example, a student who becomes overheated may have seizure activity, or music in the oversized gym may be overly stimulating for the student with autism who has sensory issues. Paraeducators know how to handle various issues related to the students' behaviors and limitations. In addition, they can be depended upon to research questions or concerns that the general physical educator may have regarding the inclusion of students with disabilities. They are also in contact with the physical therapist (PT) and the occupational therapist (OT) in the schools, who have valuable knowledge relating to students' particular needs.

PEER FACILITATORS

Providing the opportunity for peer facilitators to interact with students with disabilities is, in my opinion, the most important reason to include students with disabilities in general physical education. Peers provide modeling for behavior, physical skills, and socialization that students with disabilities often do not have the opportunity to gain in other facets of their day. Furthermore, research has shown that all children derive more value socially from other children than they could ever obtain from interacting with adults.

Using general students to facilitate in general physical education may often be left to the discretion of the physical educator. Initially, the student with a disability may attend general physical education under the assistance of a paraeducator, and general students may not be engaged in the inclusive process. If this is the circumstance, I recommend that the physical education teacher and the paraeducator work together to engage peer facilitators.

In my experience, involving peer facilitators in elementary schools has been a natural process. Some students instinctively gravitate to the students with disabilities and are great innate facilitators. Perhaps this is due to the lack of peer pressure or inhibitions or to a desire to help others and to please the teacher. Nonetheless, my experiences have been more positive than negative.

▶ Peer facilitation is a mutually beneficial process.

In some situations, I have engaged the shy or overweight student who appeared to have few friends and have been amazed at how the student's self-esteem improved. In other circumstances, I have chosen students who tend to be more active and have difficulty following directions and have been equally amazed at the improvement in their behavior when they are given the responsibility of helping others. In all of these situations, the paraeducator provided support to the peer facilitator during the process, and eventually the paraeducator was able to fade the support and allow the students to interact. Inclusion has proven to be a powerful influence for all students involved in this process.

Likewise, in the middle and high school settings, I have approached students who did not dress out for the day and asked them to assist students with disabilities and have been pleasantly surprised. Some of these students continued to assist the students with disabilities for the remainder of the course and were motivated to dress out each day. However, without programs that facilitate peer relationships for students with disabilities, middle school students seem to be the group least likely to volunteer. Creating some type of peer facilitation group would ensure better participation.

Using general students to peer facilitate in the self-contained environment is often called *reverse mainstreaming* and has proven to be very effective in my school system. All students with and without disabilities benefit from this type of inclusion, which enables the students with disabilities to receive more hands-on support from the general students. In a reverse-mainstream situation, the peer facilitators come into a self-contained environment to assist students with disabilities; or in my school system, they follow the students into a general education setting. This individual or personal attention creates a situation in which the students with disabilities are more motivated to participate. Many other schools now train peer facilitators specifically for this purpose.

I have taken peer facilitation in a different direction and developed what I call *inter-exceptionality inclusion.* By this I mean the inclusion of different levels of intellectual disabilities in one classroom. Normally, ID (intellectual disabilities) groups are scheduled by level of ID. With inter-exceptionality inclusion, I sometimes group a MID (mild) with a MOID (moderate) group or a MOID group with a SID/PID (severe/profound) group, which represents inclusion of students with lower levels in a group of students with higher levels. I have noticed that the higher-level students in each scenario act as the peer facilitators for the lower group. With this grouping, I am seeing increased self-esteem and skill improvement in the higher-functioning students. The lower groups eventually tend to model appropriate behavior and perform some skills that they were unable to perform earlier.

I would recommend that any adapted physical educator use inter-exceptionality inclusion when the scheduling opportunity presents itself. In my school system, the special education teachers in all of our middle and high schools train groups of peer facilitators through a course that the students are allowed to sign up for. They call the peer facilitator groups "Friends" or the "Friends Club." These peer facilitators learn the characteristics of various disabilities and ways to interact age appropriately with the students that they are assisting, and they are even exposed to community outreach programs within their areas. In addition, the peer facilitators learn valuable communication and interpersonal skills, ways to observe and problem solve, and responsible decision-making and leadership skills. Once trained, the peer facilitators assist the students in inclusive situations such as homeroom, music, art, physical education, computer sessions, and lunch. In addition, they may attend Special Olympics events or go on other special field trips. The two people instrumental in starting this incredible program in our schools were Gayle Allen (gayle.allen@cherokee.k12.ga.us) and Donna Ratliff (Donna.ratliff@cherokee.k12.ga.us), and they will gladly answer any questions that you may have.

If your school does not have a peer facilitation program, which would most likely be run by the counselors, I suggest that you approach the counselors or special education teachers in your school for guidance. If they are not aware of the possibilities, they will definitely be advocates for the development of such programs. Also, the teachers in my school system have used the books *Peer Helping–A Training Guide, The Peer Helper's Pocketbook,* and *Peer Buddy Programs for Successful Secondary School Inclusion,* as well as Special Education Resources on the Internet (SERI) (www.seriweb.com/).

Again, it is important to train the peer facilitators properly to ensure the best results for all students involved. Each chapter of this book includes suggestions for peer facilitation based on the differing abilities of the students needing assistance. The following guidelines present an overall view of the skills that need to be addressed for all peer facilitators. In addition, regardless of the roles that the peer facilitators are asked to assume, it is important to remember that these peers require ongoing support and encouragement.

- Teach peers to use age-appropriate behavior when interacting with students who have disabilities. Students with disabilities should not be treated like babies. Younger students with intellectual disabilities are often fine with this, but students with no cognitive delays are not.

- Inform peers that they are not allowed to physically lift students from wheelchairs, mats, or the floor. This includes helping students in wheelchairs get in or out of the wheelchair.

- Train peers to allow the student being assisted to do as much as possible without assistance.

- Encourage peers to be gently persistent during interactions. They should repeat questions and comments and not give up prematurely.

- Coach peers to provide adequate time for students to process and respond to information, especially when assisting students with autism.

- Inform the peers that it is acceptable to say "no" or "stop" when students display inappropriate behaviors. However, it is the responsibility of the teacher or paraeducator to discipline any student.

- Teach peers basic sign language needed to interact with students who are nonverbal. Words such as *stop, go, yes, no,* and *thank you* are a starting point.

- Encourage the peer facilitators to become advocates for students with disabilities. Suggest that they speak up when students with disabilities are being left out or become the target of jeers from others.

A more specific skill to teach peer facilitators, as well as some paraeducators, relates to the hierarchy of prompts. Many of our students with disabilities depend on verbal or physical prompts to get started in an activity because of motor or cognitive delays. The following prompts recommended by the special education teachers in my school system have been successful with my students.

1. Independent: Allow the student time to respond on his or her own.
2. Verbal: Give the student a verbal prompt and allow time to respond.
3. Gestural: This is a nonverbal direction, with the paraeducator or peer performing the skill for the student to model. Pointing is another nonverbal gesture that students respond to.
4. Physical: Actually assist the student hand over hand, or lead the student with touch.

Some students will need one or more of these prompts for each attempt at a skill, while some need no prompts at all. The goal is to provide the prompts and work toward reducing the number of prompts that the student will need in order to work independently. However, understand that this is a process and that it is necessary to provide time and experiences for the process to occur.

Including all students is not always a simple task, but utilizing the paraeducators and peer facilitators can contribute to a favorable outcome for all involved.

CONCLUSION

Part of our hidden curriculum as physical educators is to provide a safe and secure environment that focuses on the success of all students of all abilities; thus relying on support is acceptable and necessary when we are trying to include all students. My suggestion for all physical educators is to utilize all members of the staff to maintain inclusion as a natural and progressive part of your program. Use your resources, whether those are OT, PT, the special education teacher, administrators, parents, other physical educators, paraeducators, or peer facilitators, and make a difference in the lives of others. Most importantly, build a positive relationship with the student who has a disability, as well as the support staff, and receive the many benefits of participating in these relationships.

INCLUDING STUDENTS WITH AUTISM SPECTRUM DISORDER

Physical education has the potential to be a valuable tool for including students with autism. Engaging in leisure activities and play, as well as learning social skills, enhances any child's quality of life. A quality physical education environment provides socialization, which the student with autism is lacking. Also it helps develop gross motor skills for the student with autism who may have delays. For students with autism who have few delays in motor development, physical education can be the realm in which the student stands out when accompanying peers. Even more simply, learning to stand in line teaches the student some degree of independence. Physical educators need only to learn a few techniques, have a little patience, and be open to changes in order to include these students.

Any structured program that works on skill development can include students with disabilities, especially students with autism. It is to the student's advantage if he or she can be included early in elementary school in order to address sensory and communication issues as soon as possible. This is also an important point given that general peers seem more tolerant at younger ages. Research has proven that peers perform a role in socialization that adults cannot duplicate. Typically developing students model a whole different type of empathy, friendship, and acceptance. Therefore, early intervention is profoundly necessary for inclusion of students with autism.

UNDERSTANDING
AUTISM SPECTRUM DISORDER

As the term "spectrum" implies, a wide range of cognitive, communication, and social abilities is represented in children with autism. The diagnosis ranges from autism with varying degrees of cognitive, social, and communication disabilities to Asperger syndrome, in which the student has normal intelligence and language development but has deficiencies in social and pragmatic skills (Ervin, 2007). Still, most children with autism have some level of intellectual delay and speech and language problems. Some of these children do not speak; others have limited language skills; and others use repetitive phrases. Yet most experts agree that it is the physical and emotional detachment from other people and the severe communication difficulties that are the hallmark symptoms of autism (Richard, 1997).

What works for one student with autism may or may not work for another. A technique that works for a student today may not work tomorrow. There is no "mold" for the child with autism. Therefore, it is imperative to be patient and open to trying new things.

Students with autism need to keep reviewing information to help them remember. It is of great importance as an educator to choose the skill or behavior that you want to teach the student and break that skill into smaller increments. Then, add new information as the student masters each skill.

Many students with autism have very acute senses. Noise, touch, or even bright lights can often overstimulate them, causing them to display stereotypical autistic behaviors such as extended gazing, flapping, rocking, twirling, or spinning (Ervin, 2007). This self-stimulating behavior is usually a sign that the child is under stress. If the student starts the self-stimulating behavior during any activity, slow down the activity or take the child to the side, and the self-stimulating behavior should slow down. Using a timer at this point will sometimes help the student calm down a little faster. Also, the student may need to walk around the gym to calm down.

In addition, some students with autism have hypoactive (underresponsive) senses (National Center on Physical Activity and Disability [NCPAD], 2008). In these cases, students can become self-injurious (e.g., engage in head banging, biting, or scratching) when frustrated or overstimulated. When this occurs, the teacher or paraeducator should intervene to stop the behavior. For example, sometimes adding an alternate activity to engage the student will help him or her refocus and stop the behavior. In some extreme cases, the student may need to be removed from the classroom or gym.

Sensory problems may make it difficult for the student to initially participate in physical education or even to enter the gym. So, allow participation in differing degrees or steps, for example, (1) arrive at the gym, (2) next, sit in the corner, (3) then participate only in warm-ups, and (4) eventually do an activity. Some students may start participating at the third or fourth level; others may stay at the first level for weeks. The key is to allow the student the time and modifications necessary for success at any level.

In some cases, the student with sensory issues may need to wear a weighted vest or may need compression strategies. If this is the case, the paraeducator will have been trained to provide what is needed. Most importantly, the school's occupational therapist (OT) has a formula to determine the amount of weight in the vest and can provide additional strategies and techniques for sensory issues. The general educator needs only to be open to allowing the use of these strategies in the classroom and to realize that once the sensory issues are addressed, the student's behavior more often than not improves.

On the other hand, some students with autism are sensitive to touch and do not tolerate even the slightest contact from others, even hugs. These students will have a difficult time holding hands in a game, so it may be helpful to provide an object such as a rubber ring or a rope held by another student for the student with autism to grasp, or to avoid holding hands altogether. Also, some students with autism may not be able to tolerate being tagged in a game of chase. In this case, I would ask the general students to avoid tagging the student. This was the case for one of my students, but he and the other students handled the problem without assistance. The student with autism would say "beep, beep" as others approached him for the tag, and the general students just knew instinctively not to tag him. I figured this out by observing and asking the students about it.

Additionally, ordinary things such as clothing tags or scratchy material in clothing can irritate a student and cause him or her to become agitated. The paraeducator will be aware of these circumstances with the student and will often handle the issue before it becomes a problem. Once again, the general educator needs to be open to strategies carried out by the paraeducator to address these sensory issues.

Be prepared for distractions from students with sensory struggles, and inform the general peers that some things may need to be ignored. In the initial stages of inclusion, you should be ready to teach over these distractions and understand that improvement will be seen over time. Be patient and focus on the process.

Learning strategies to decrease negative behaviors and increase positive behaviors is critical when you are teaching students with autism. I have found that it is more effective for most students with autism to work toward a positive reinforcement rather than having things taken away because of negative behaviors. This strategy keeps the student in a positive state and motivates the student to perform given tasks. Too often, I have seen students with autism become upset and almost defiant when things such as computer, recess, or free time are taken away because they did not do what was asked of them. Accentuate the positive for positive results.

With this in mind, note that students with autism have significant difficulty expressing their thoughts and desires in an effective manner. For example, sometimes the purpose of a negative behavior is to gain attention, or a behavior may be an attempt to communicate. Knowing this, the paraeducator or the teacher can help others understand some of the student's confusing behaviors. Communication between the teacher, paraprofessional, and family members is necessary to help the student transition more effectively and be a part of the general classroom. This is truly a team effort, and the student responds better when all adults are on the same page and have the same expectations, whether at home or at school.

Strategies for Inclusion

The following are some basic strategies that I have found useful when including students with autism in my general or self-contained classrooms. Many of the strategies are for communication, socialization, or sensory issues, which cause most of the challenges for students with autism. Along with these strategies, a consistent class routine is needed each day, such as warm-ups, activity, and closing. This routine provides expectations for the student, which in turn relieves stress. All strategies will not work for every student, and most strategies are used in conjunction with others. So, be prepared to try different approaches to reach different students with autism, and try different strategies should one fail for a particular student.

Emphasize Social Interaction

Refining social skills of students with autism should be a primary and ongoing goal. Use peer facilitators as often as possible. Any chance to interact with general peers is invaluable to the child with autism. General students model behaviors and skills that the student with autism is lacking. As stated earlier, these peers provide friendship and acceptance that the student with autism has limited opportunity to receive because outside programs are limited for all children with disabilities. However, opportunities for children with disabilities are increasing because more and more recreation and leisure programs are aware of the need.

Another significant motive for the use of peer facilitators is to reduce the student's dependence on the paraeducator or any other adult associated with the student. Studies have shown that students with autism often respond well to adults but sometimes become too dependent on an adult for motivation. Therefore, there is a great need for interactions with general peers. Once the student starts to interact with peers, more and more opportunity is available for the student to be included.

With this in mind, when including students with autism in general physical education, understand that it is necessary and appropriate to inform and educate the general population in the classroom. Start by explaining that some students have a difficult time following directions because they do not understand and that they will need extra help and modifications. Introduce some of the possible behaviors, such as rocking or humming, that the student with autism may exhibit because of overstimulation or frustration. Let the students know that this behavior is not bad, but that the student with autism will need extra help or a few rule changes. Inform the general students that they should not be overly concerned if the student with autism breaks a few rules—that the student will get better at understanding rules as the class progresses.

It is common for peers to assume that students with autism are unfriendly when they do not respond to questions or greetings. Therefore, it is helpful to give peers specific instructions for interacting with students with autism. Give specific directions to the peer helper working one-on-one with the student, such as the need to be gently persistent during interactions, and encourage the peer to provide adequate time for the student with autism to process the information. It is paramount to provide instructions about what the peer should do if the student with autism begins to show aggression. Dealing with negative or aggressive behavior should never be the responsibility of the peer, but let the peer know that it is acceptable to say "no" or "stop."

It is equally important to point out the strengths of the student with autism to enable the general students to become more accepting and tolerant and less afraid of the unknown. Unless the general peers have the opportunity to interact with the student with autism, they are unaware of some of the incredible skills or talents that the student may have to offer. For example, I have had students with autism in elementary classes read locomotor cards for the rest of the class and watched the amazed faces of the general students once they realized that the student was "smart enough" to read. Likewise, students of any age are always impressed when the student with autism demonstrates a particular skill such as striking, batting, and kicking or answers a question concerning rules or regulations.

ENCOURAGE STAYING ON TASK

Most students with autism need more clearly defined and understandable boundaries when participating in group activities. I have found that spot markers (poly spots) work remarkably well for helping the student with autism stay on task or with the group. When first incorporating the spot, you may have to keep redirecting the student to the spot. Sometimes it takes days or weeks to get the student to stay on

▶ Peer assisting a student standing on his "spot."

the spot, but continue redirecting. It will be worth the effort once the student is able to focus and participate. General peers can also learn to redirect the student with autism back to the spot marker.

Spot markers can be used as a personal space or in games or relays that require the student to move from one side of the court to the other. If you have several students with autism in your classroom, use a different-colored spot for each student and refer to the color of the spot when directing the student to the spot. Some students may even need a spot to stand on when participating in centers or stations. This is a perfect situation to allow peers to redirect the student back to his or her spot if needed. This will allow the student the opportunity to work with a partner one-on-one. In some cases, that same student may even need prompting from the paraeducator or teacher to interact and participate with the peer. Ultimately, some students will no longer need a spot to stay on task.

My students with autism continue to prove the value of using a spot marker. For example, I had an elementary student who needed a spot on a regular basis; otherwise he would run around the gym aimlessly. On one particular day the class activity was tumbling, so I provided the spot marker to enable him to stand in line. As I scanned the room, I noticed that he was running around the gym and that his spot was no longer in the area where I had placed it. I figured out that he had hidden the spot marker under one of the mats. Once I retrieved it and instructed him to return to the spot, he rejoined his classmates. However, I did have to continuously monitor him to keep him from throwing or hiding his spot. This effort was worthwhile, though, because it enabled him to be included.

If the student with autism has difficulty sitting for instructions and the spot does not seem to help, allow the student to walk around the gym with the paraeducator or a general peer during this time. Provide a sideline activity such as squeezing a sensory ball to help the student stay calm. Some students may need to enter the gym only after instructions have been given because it is too difficult for them to sit and focus during this time.

ADAPT COMMUNICATION

Individuals with autism have problems processing; therefore abstract thinking is difficult for them. They tend to be literal and need concrete or specific means of communication. Some students with autism have problems with pronoun reversals and often refer to themselves by their proper names rather than saying "me" or "I" (Richard, 1997). Given this, I have found that they respond well to someone speaking to them in third person; this seems to immediately gain their attention. For example, I might say "Joe can catch," instead of "Catch, Joe." This may also help in redirecting the student with autism to his or her spot. For example, I might say "This is Joe's spot" or "Joe goes to the red spot." Speaking in third person is also helpful in turn-taking situations; for example, "It is Joe's turn" may let Joe know that it's his turn or may prompt him to do whatever skill you are asking him to perform. As the student develops better language skills, I speak in third person only if needed in order for the student to process the information.

As another example of a situation in which speaking in third person has been successful, a student who likes to sit on the floor may refuse to stand up when asked to do so. I will say "Susie can stand up" or "Susie is ready to stand up"; after a few seconds I will add "Susie can stand up." Usually the student stands up. However, sometimes I have to wait 5 to 10 seconds and say it again. Then she stands up. If this does not work, I bring a chair to her and prompt her to sit in the chair; then we work on standing up.

Higher-functioning students with better language skills may be reluctant to have someone speak to them in third person. For example, a middle school student with Asperger syndrome who refused to follow directions asked me, in his words, to "stop speaking in that third-person thing." I explained to him that I did this only when he did not follow the rules. (I had never explained the third-person strategy to him.) We made an agreement that I would speak in third person only when he was not following directions. The positive change in his behavior was remarkable. The incident proved to me how incredibly powerful this strategy is for the student with autism.

Finally, when time is one of those absolutes that the student with autism understands or depends on, it is necessary to prepare the student for transition from one activity to the next or for the end of the class period. For example, the teacher may announce that there is 1 minute left before the activity stops, or that there is 1 minute left in class. Likewise, if the school day schedule is interrupted, it is wise to announce to the student that "around or about 9:00," physical education will start or end. For the student preoccupied with time, any change in the schedule can cause panic or extreme confusion. Any unexpected change can ruin the student's day.

Telling the student that he has three more bats, kicks, or throws will also make for a smoother transition from one activity to the next. In addition, I often inform the student of the next expected behavior or event by saying, "Now, Josh will go to the circle to get ready to leave." This takes only a small amount of effort but can make an improbably great difference for the student with autism who struggles with transition.

Using *consistent language* is another strategy of great importance. For example, use one word for stop or freeze, but not both. Use shorter sentences if you perceive that the student is having difficulty understanding you. In addition, avoid verbal overload by having only one person giving the student directions. (The teacher and paraeducator need to work together, but they need to allow each other to speak separately.) The student can become easily overstimulated with too much noise, whether from spoken language or just from the environment of the noisy gym.

Encourage the student with autism to communicate with words. For example, ask yes or no questions and use your hands to give the student a means of answering. For example, the student can touch your right hand for "yes" and your left hand for "no." Or, provide choices with your hands to help prompt the student and to initiate communication. Also, ask the student to call the name of the person he or she is interacting with during play. If any of these strategies become agitating to the student, use them in small increments and teach the peers to interact in this manner in short increments.

Most students with autism are visual learners and can learn basic sign language that relates to physical education for communicating with others (e.g., sit, stand, go, stop, run, more, yes and no). These

▶ Sign language can be an effective tool for communicating with students with autism, who tend to be visual learners.

basic signs are simple for the peers to pick up too and can facilitate great partnerships for play.

Without general students in the classroom, it is more difficult to motivate students with autism. In a self-contained classroom they have no modeling from their general peers. When teaching this group I speak to the students primarily in third person. Usually, I have to speak directly to each student to get him or her to participate. It is hard for students with autism to start without this prompting because they often have problems interpreting body language or reading facial expressions. Without the prompting they often choose to retreat and will not interact.

ALLOW EXTRA RESPONSE TIME

Give verbal or visual directions or both (but not at the same time) to the student with autism, and allow extra time for the student to respond. Often it takes the student a bit longer to process incoming information and respond to the command. Again, allow one person at a time to interact with the student when giving directions to avoid overload. After a short delay, the student may need another prompt from the paraeducator or the peer facilitator.

A simple strategy to remember regarding the delayed response time or for prompting the student to participate is to use the formula *tell, show, do. Tell* the student what you want him or her to do, wait 5 seconds, then *show* the student what to do, wait 5 more seconds, and then *do* or physically assist the student in performing the task. This formula is especially helpful to use for students who need motivation to participate. Eventually, the delayed response time can decrease and the student will need less prompting from another individual.

USE POSITIVE REINFORCERS

Some students with autism get attached to particular types of objects and may collect items that have no apparent function but intrinsically provide enjoyment for them. Though students can become preoccupied with these objects, it is possible to use such an object to motivate the student to perform a skill or participate in an activity. For example, if the student is interested in hoops and wants to play only with hoops, allow him to use a hoop for a few minutes after he has performed a particular skill or to use the hoop for a short time before you ask him to perform a skill. Or, if the student loves dinosaurs, allow a prede-termined amount of time for her to play with her dinosaur figurine after she has completed a task. Continue using this form of motivation throughout the class time. In most cases, the paraprofessional will monitor this interaction.

Similarly, you may allow a high school student to shoot baskets for 2 minutes once he has completed a particular task. Another suggestion is to allow free time at the end of class for the student as a positive reinforcement for participating in the class activity or for following directions. Again, the paraeducator will be aware of the needed intrin-sic motivator and can monitor the student's behavior.

USE WRITTEN LANGUAGE STRATEGIES

Because most students with autism are visual learners and often need concrete approaches to learning, written language is very helpful in deepening their understanding of a task they have been asked to per-form. I have been and continue to be amazed at the magic of written language for the student with autism. It works more often than not, and the student reacts almost immediately upon reading the script.

In one situation, because written language was so powerful for one of my sixth grade students, I had to catch the student off guard, which often felt like a game of tag, to get him to read a *Social Story* (explained on page 29). He did not want to read in physical education class because, to him, that meant he would have to perform the skill described. He did not enjoy exercise, but according to his physical therapist he needed the movement to improve certain developmental motor delays. For this reason, I felt obligated to get him to participate. After reading his story, he would do whatever the story instructed.

Another student with autism who was in a team-building class refused to step on the uppermost rung of a ladder because the label on the top of the ladder read "Do not stand on top." He said, "Oh, no," then read the label out loud and refused to step on the highest rung so that he could go over the 8-foot (2.4-meter) climbing wall. The next day, I taped over the label before he attempted to climb. When he got to the top of the ladder he was obviously looking for the label and was a little surprised not to find it. With support and using the top rung, he was able to climb over the wall.

Lists Sometimes when entering a physical education class the student with autism may become overwhelmed with the size of the class, the noise level, or just the transition and then become confused about what to do. I have learned that if I list the activities for the day, the student calms down and can participate. The list does not have to be elaborate and can be written within seconds.

For example, this simple list was used to prompt a seventh grade student into entering the gym. Once he read the list, he entered the gym and participated for the first time that semester with his general peers.

1. Warm-ups
2. Team dodgeball
3. Leave

To go a step further and increase the student's participation level, we also added some specific boundaries to the game for the student. He was allowed to stand in the lane area of the court, which provided a safety base, and the other students were told that they could not throw the ball at him when he was standing in the lane area. At first, he danced in and out of the lane, but within 10 or so minutes he was running around the court and rarely used the safety area. So, once we had enlisted this student to participate, we used the second strategy of providing concrete boundaries and saw an improvement in his participation level.

Some students will need a few more specifics to be added to their list and may need to check off the activities on the list as they complete them. For example, the following list is one that I used with a student with autism who was intellectually disabled and had some behavior issues. This student needed to check off the activity to help him stay focused and to transition from one activity to the next. He actually marked through each line with a pencil when moving from one station to the next, and some days we used a timer to help him keep track of the time he spent in each station. On other days, use of the timer proved frustrating to him and we avoided it.

Warm-ups: running, stretching	10 minutes
First station: scoops and balls	10 minutes
Second station: dribbling	10 minutes
Third station: scooters	10 minutes
Line up to leave	

You may also write the listed items on separate index cards and collect each card as the student finishes the activity. Index cards can be used in the same way to tally laps during walking or running. Both provide clear expectations for the student.

Pictures   Students who cannot read respond well to pictures. Pictures can be used in various ways. You can arrange pictures of activities in columns and fasten them to a board with Velcro; the student chooses an activity by pulling one of the pictures off the board. Or the student can move the pictures from one column to another after completing the given activities. The paraeducator will usually provide the picture board if necessary, especially if the special education teachers use the board in the classroom, or you can create your own. I often use Writing with Symbols 2000 or cut and paste pictures from books, magazines, or the computer. For examples of a visual stick, which is smaller and less involved, see chapter 6.

Social Stories   Other students with autism may need more direction and respond well to *Social Stories*. Social Stories are simple stories dealing with social events and situations that are difficult for students with autism to understand. The stories describe situations with a focus on social cues and on expected behaviors of the student with autism, and can give perspective on the thoughts and emotions of others (Wallin, 2009). Basically, Social Stories are a tool for teaching social skills to children with autism and other disabilities.

I have used Social Stories with my students for behavior management, for skill performance, and for social situations, as well as to teach class rules or to calm a student. The stories suggest appropriate responses in different situations and help improve the student's comfort level. My students with autism who have intellectual disabilities, as well as students with Asperger syndrome, respond well to Social Stories.

Social Stories were developed by Carol Gray. Should you feel the need to obtain more information about them, her book *The New Social Story Book,* and her Web site, www.thegraycenter.org, are excellent resources that will give you access to sample stories. I have also acquired very instructive information on the Web site www.polyxo .com.

When using Social Stories, I have the student read the story as soon as he or she enters the gym. The stories can also be effective when read to the student. Often, if the student refuses to read the story, I start reading it and eventually the student joins in. Students who are not responding to the story appropriately may need to reread it several times during a physical education session. At times, I've had to rewrite the story several times before the student actually understood it. For this reason, I keep a folder of all Social Stories that I use for each student and reuse them for particular skills, lesson plans, or behaviors in order to avoid rewriting stories.

Some higher-functioning students may need a story only when a problem arises. For example, a student with Asperger syndrome may need a story for a problem with socialization only on a particular day with regard to a particular person or circumstance. Another student could be upset about something that happened in an earlier class and may need a story to help him or her refocus. As you can see, the stories can be used at different times, and you will need to figure out the best formula for your students.

Gray's Social Stories can be used in many situations in your classes and they can be rewritten to fit your students' specific needs. However, as a general physical educator, I often found it more effective to write my own social stories on the spot. For example, if a behavior problem occurred or a student became over-stimulated, or if a student did not understand certain rules, I needed a story at that moment and it was easier to write the story than to try to find one in a book.

Social Stories may seem like a lot of work, but once you get the hang of writing them they are a very valuable tool for decreasing negative behaviors and increasing positive behaviors. I once asked a parent how important Social Stories were for her child, and she shared that they were *imperative* and that they created success for him. She believed that he could not have gotten through elementary school without them, and she added that she and his teachers used the stories for every aspect of his education. She also mentioned that as a high school student, he still needed a Social Story on rare occasions and responded well to them. He was also able to walk from class to class on his own and played on a Special Olympics basketball team.

In my experience in writing Social Stories, these are the things that I have found useful. I try to include one or two descriptive sentences and two or three directive sentences as suggested by Gray and others, as well as writing the story in first person. I try to phrase sentences in order to avoid the word "not." I have found that the student with autism will sometimes skip over the word "not," and this obviously changes the meaning of the sentence. Considering that some students with autism refer to themselves by their proper name, I always start the social story with "My name is _____." For the student with no pronoun reversal problems, it has proven beneficial to start the student's Social Story in the same way. You will not see this particular element in Carol Gray's books, but I have found it helpful for my students. However, for my higher functioning students, sometimes I just write their name at the top of the Social Story and this has worked for those students. I have even had students ask me to write their names on the story for them.

As you will notice in the stories in figure 2.1, I have not included everything that the student will be doing during the class period. I give the student enough information to increase understanding or to make the student more comfortable. Often, I try to consider the cause-and-effect situation of each game, activity, behavior, or social scenario that the student may have difficulty with and include a statement or two about that. For example, some students have problems with being tagged and being "out" in a game, so I let these students know that it is okay to get tagged and often include a sentence to convey to them that they are "out" for only a short amount of time. This has proven more effective for my students than actually writing the rules of the game or activity.

Sometimes I write more than one story for a student. If a story is needed for a behavior problem, I write a short story about participation first. I feel this starts the student in a positive state. Then, on a second sheet of paper I write the behavior modification story. Both stories are short and to the point in an effort to avoid overloading the student with too much information. Again, I save the stories in a folder to use whenever needed.

INCLUDING STUDENTS WITH SEVERE AUTISM

Including students on the more severe end of the autism spectrum can prove to be a greater challenge. Some of these students may have

Skill Development and Participation

My name is Joe. Today in PE, I will be playing games. Sometimes I will be running. Sometimes I will be walking. Sometimes I will be sitting in line. I will have fun and follow the rules.

My name is Joe. Today in PE, I will be playing soccer with the big ball. Sometimes I will crab walk and kick the ball. Sometimes I will sit on the line and kick the ball. I will use my feet instead of my hands.

My name is Joe. Today in PE, I will be playing bombardi. Bombardi is a very fun game. All kids love to play bombardi. I will try to knock down the pins. If I hit another kid with the ball, he or she is out. If I get hit, I will be out. When the game is over, I will play again.

My name is Joe. Today in PE, I will be playing with hoops. Sometimes I will balance in my hoop. Sometimes I will hop in my hoop. My teacher will tell me how to play with my hoop. I will have fun.

▶ Figure 2.1 Sample Social Stories.

Behavior Modification

My name is Joe. I will stop running in the bleachers. I will stay off the mats. When the teacher is talking, I will listen. I will stop making noises with my mouth. (This is a story written to help the student decrease negative behaviors.)

My name is Joe. Meghan is my friend. Meghan says for me to stop smashing, bumping, or colliding into her. If I keep doing these things, Meghan will stop being my friend. I must stop touching Meghan in any way. It is OK for Meghan to play with other kids. (This story was written for a student who perseverates on another student. The words used in the story were words that the student uses. This student was a higher-functioning student with autism.)

▶ Figure 2.1 *(continued)*

heightened sensory struggles, self-injurious behaviors, aggressive behaviors toward others, attention deficit disorders, or some combination of these. All of the strategies mentioned previously are possible tools, but it may take longer for them to become effective and they may not be modifiable to a suitable degree. In these cases, I have used what I term *guided participation and intervention*. This plan also works in conjunction with a student's behavioral intervention plan (BIP).

This process provides a support system to help maximize the student's developmental potential. It requires a paraeducator to introduce the student into the classroom and to monitor behavior to determine when the student is prepared to become more involved. The objective is to increase participation in small increments and then to improve social skills through gradual interaction with individuals and then the group. The goal is sequential; that is, we first aim to increase participation and then work on improving social skills by slowly engaging other students.

Implementing Participation

- Use a consistent class routine: warm-ups, activity or activities, and closing. These consistent routines are necessary and provide expected outcomes that can potentially require less intervention from the instructor.

- The student will enter the gym with no expectation on the part of others that he or she will participate. The student with sensory problems or aggressive or self-injurious behavior may be able to stay in the noisy environment of the gym for only a few minutes initially. Time is increased in small increments, and no expectations for participation are placed on the student.

- Once the student is able to tolerate the environment, provide a "spot marker" for the student to stand on to provide a designated area of consistency. A few students may be able to accept peer interaction at this point, but the main goal is participation.

- Add prompts to perform skills (warm-ups or activity for the day). This may need to start separately from the group. If so, inform the general students that the student with autism does not need intervention from them yet. It may be necessary to go to the student to introduce any skill or activity, such as striking or kicking a ball, and provide this instruction on the sidelines of the gym.

- Always provide positive reinforcement using feedback or high fives.

- Use a list or a social story, if the student can read, to provide guidelines for behavior.

- Use picture cards of the activity or preferred behavior if the student cannot read. These work well for the younger student or a student with more cognitive delays.

Integrating Socialization

- The student enters the gym; there is no interaction with peers.
- Interaction without touch begins; for example, a peer will be allowed to give positive feedback or to compliment the student and walk away.
- Eventually, another student will give a high five and then walk away.
- A peer partner is incorporated, with adult supervision and at a reasonable distance from the student, starting with 10 to 12 feet (3 to 3.7 meters). The paraeducator will need to guide social exchanges.
- Adult supervision is faded when the student is ready. This time varies for each student.

Socialization may need to be added when participation has reached a reasonable level. Even if the student is not socializing with others, just being in the same environment allows the student with autism to observe modeled behaviors from the general students, which he or she may eventually start to duplicate. Fading instructor supervision is at the discretion of the instructor and will be based on the fact that the problem behaviors have subsided enough to allow the student to stay in the gym without mishap.

STRUCTURED
PHYSICAL EDUCATION OPPORTUNITIES

Any physical education program that provides opportunities for students to play cooperative games, allows them to develop skills through drills or repetition, utilizes lead-up games and sports, and supports rhythm and dance, as well as lifetime recreational activities and fitness training, will be appropriate for including students with autism. These programs can promote success for all learners, especially if individual differences are considered and modifications are implemented.

In addition, stations or centers in elementary and middle school physical education programs are excellent for including students with autism and provide necessary peer interaction. In these centers, the students have the opportunity to make choices and develop social and motor skills. Refer to chapter 7 for suggested activities.

In the upper elementary, middle, or high school programs where team sports are introduced, some students with autism may not be able to participate; and it is recommended that these students participate with a peer in a parallel activity on the sideline. Or, add an extra rule or step to the game specifically for the student with autism. For example, during a flag football game, have the student with autism throw a ball through or into a target as a bonus point after the team has scored. In the meantime, the student can participate in a one-on-one or two-on-two drill of football skills with peers. But consider that many students will be able to participate with peer interaction and guidance. It may be necessary to provide a separate area for dressing out, or the student may need to be excused from dressing out all together.

CONCLUSION

Including students with autism can be a challenging, but rewarding, experience. Once you are aware that these students have struggles with socialization, communication, and sensory issues, you have taken the first step in the process. Remember that most students with autism are visual learners and benefit from the use of written language such as Social Stories and lists. They need concrete boundaries such as spot markers or designated areas for play. Be prepared to use multiple strategies and to change or modify these strategies when needed.

Most importantly, be open to providing a safe and embracing environment that includes general peers to model appropriate behaviors and motor skills. Physical education is often one of the first settings utilized for inclusion because of the positive outcomes. We should be proud of that fact and know that our efforts will be appreciated.

Including Students Who Use Wheelchairs

Students who use wheelchairs will surprise and amaze you. They are eager to participate, and they gain tremendous good from the general students. Likewise, the general students learn many intrinsic values as peer helpers and become more empathetic, patient, and caring individuals when given the opportunity to peer facilitate. They also improve communication skills that are important in all aspects of their lives. It is a give-and-take situation for both the students with exceptionalities and the able-bodied peers.

Your students using wheelchairs will vary greatly in cognitive ability. As a general rule, students in wheelchairs with the same cognitive abilities as the able-bodied students prefer to do the things that the general physical education class is doing. Not all students will perform at the same levels; there are varying degrees of participation, so it is key to adjust adaptations according to the student's level of mobility and upper body strength. Students with upper body strength and control will be able to perform more activities independently than a student with less upper body strength or control. The student with limited or no upper body control will depend on the paraprofessional or peer helper to become successful.

Sometimes educators get caught up in the overall goal of having all students perform at the same level. But it's important to help all students patiently to perform at their ability level. Particularly with students with disabilities, educators must focus on the strength of each student and build on it. When planning, your main focus should be on what the student can do instead of what the student cannot do. In addition, if the activity for the student with the disability is remotely related to what the general students are doing, the student with the disability will feel included.

It is important when adjusting the rules for the student in a wheelchair to convey these rules to the rest of the physical education class so that everyone understands all safety aspects. You do not need to explain the student's condition, just the rule change; and if a safety issue is involved, the general students need to be informed about it. I make it a point to ask the student's permission before announcing a safety rule to the group. However, if safety is the main concern and the student in the wheelchair is not comfortable with my sharing safety rules with the rest of the class, I provide another activity for the student on the sideline. For example, some students have conditions that are additional or secondary to being in a wheelchair, such as shunts that are not always obvious to the untrained eye, and should never receive a blow to the head. Tag games, games in which balls are thrown at others, or games in which balls need to be rebounded would be dangerous for a student with a shunt unless there were some safety precautions or modifications. These will be discussed throughout the chapter.

Sometimes rule changes are made to "even the playing field" for the student in a wheelchair; examples are allowing more tags or allowing the student in the wheelchair to use shorter base-running paths. In this case, I just get permission from the student to inform the others so that they are not confused about the rule changes. I've never had a student who was uncomfortable with this. However, I do not talk about the student's disability. In addition, I caution others to be aware of students in wheelchairs and to watch out for them when fleeing or dodging in games.

It is highly recommended that you speak with the classroom teacher or Individual Education Plan (IEP) holder or with your student's paraeducator in order to discuss any restrictions for the student. As noted in chapter 1, these personnel will have knowledge of any element of concern based on the individual's needs. They may not have the knowledge to make the modifications needed in your physical education setting, but they will be receptive and open to instituting any needed modifications based on your experience.

The restrictions for students in wheelchairs can vary based on the student's individual condition. For example, because of problems with muscular strength and fatigue, it may be necessary to limit participation for the student with muscular dystrophy. The student with spina bifida who has a shunt should avoid activities that could result in blows to the head. The student with athetoid or spastic cerebral palsy may need pervasive support at all times because of an inability to control movement and to grasp or let go of objects. Experience has shown me that understanding the conditions that circumscribe the use of a wheelchair is one of the most important factors in the process of successfully including these students.

Last, any educator or paraeducator working with any student in a wheelchair needs to become familiar with the student's chair. For all students in a wheelchair, the waist belt must be buckled at all times until the student exits the chair. For students with no upper body control or trunk stability, the shoulder straps that support the student in the chair must be buckled. For the student with a tray on the chair, it is usually permissible to remove the tray during physical education, but it is recommended that you check with the supporting educator for approval.

Most importantly, remember that no student is allowed to assist or lift someone who is transferring into or out of the chair. This is the responsibility of the paraeducator who has been trained to perform this procedure. Also, be aware that some students in wheelchairs will be able to perform skills out of their chairs. I recommend that the paraeducator use a gait belt to help steady the student, especially if the student is attempting to walk around in the area. The brakes on the wheelchair must be in the locked position when a student is transferring into or out of the chair and when the student is in a fixed position for a skill or activity.

In my school system, general students are not allowed to push other students in wheelchairs. I think this is important as a general rule, but I recognize that when general students are allowed to push the student in the wheelchair in the hallway as people are moving about the building to change classes or to go to lunch, this allows time for students to interact and get to know each other. My suggestion is that if this is allowed, the paraeducator or teacher should be within close proximity in case a problem arises.

MODIFICATIONS FOR STUDENTS WITH UPPER BODY CONTROL

Students with wheelchairs can be included in all kinds of physical education activities, from station activities to sports to skill practice, with some creative adaptations. The student's level of upper body control greatly influences the activities that he or she will be able to perform, as well as the degree to which the student will need assistance from the paraeducator or peer facilitator. Use your imagination, with your particular students' needs in mind. The following ideas might spark your own creativity.

Tag Games

- Allow the student in the wheelchair to accumulate two or more tags before he or she is eliminated or is "it."

- For ball tag games, instruct other students that in order to tag the student in a wheelchair, they must tag the back wheels of the chair by rolling the ball. You may even choose to appoint a peer helper to deflect balls for the student if needed. Never allow balls to be thrown at the student's body, especially the head.

- Place a fun noodle in the student's chair (or allow the student to hold the noodle) so that it protrudes out when the student in the chair is "it." This allows the student to push (or be pushed) and still be able to tag without getting too close to the runner, and reduces the risk that the student in the chair will run over other students.

Throwing and Catching

- For passing drills, use peer students to partner with the student in a wheelchair. Give these peer students guidelines for safety and also participation goals. Teach the peer helpers to bounce pass the ball to the student in the wheelchair so that the ball lands in the student's lap. Then the student in the wheelchair actually catches the ball by trapping it in his or her lap. This is a relatively complex skill for the peer, especially for a younger student. Therefore, initially both students will need to practice this skill. It may be necessary to use a spot marker for the peer to aim the bounce at, and the paraeducator or teacher may need to prompt the student in the wheelchair to hold his or her arms up, if possible, while waiting for the bounce. Most students will have a delayed response time when attempting to catch and will need this verbal prompt.

- Provide a box for the student with less upper body strength or control to catch with. Just placing the box or bucket in the student's lap will give the peer a target to throw to, and the student in the wheelchair will feel successful. Also, at this point the paraeducator will need to help the student return the throw with the hand-over-hand technique if the student is unable to throw or release the ball.

- Use a bowling ramp for the student to use to roll the ball to a peer when throwing is too difficult. In comparison to the hand-over-hand technique of assistance, this gives the student a little more independence.

- Use a slightly deflated beach ball. This will be softer and easier to pull into the body.

Basketball

- Allow the student in the wheelchair to hold the ball in his or her lap when dribbling. The student gets three pushes and then has to pass or shoot. Eventually, the student may be able to perform a regular dribble. A regular dribble is often difficult for the student in the wheelchair, but I have had students who learn to dribble over time. I start teaching this skill by allowing the student to push the ball out of my hands and then receive the ball as it bounces up. Eventually the student is asked to practice the drill by bouncing the ball with two hands and catching it in as many successful attempts as possible. Then the student is introduced to the one-hand dribble using the dominant hand.

- For shooting, use a lower portable goal on the sideline, or a trash can, box, or large ball cart as the goal on the sideline. Allow peer helpers to rebound and pass back.
- Do not allow a student with a shunt to participate in activities that require rebounding of the basketball. Provide another sideline activity such as those listed in the next section of this chapter.
- If the student is unable to participate in team play, add an activity for the student after each score. For example, the student could take a bonus shot for alternating teams at a lower goal, drop a ball or beanbag in a bucket, or roll the ball at a pin to knock it down.

Soccer

- Allow the student in a wheelchair to shoot or pass with his or her hands.
- Allow a peer to retrieve balls for the student in the chair if needed.
- Use lead-up games or drills for the whole class that will also enable the student in the chair to take a turn with modifications. See sample games in chapters 4 and 7.
- If the student in the chair chooses to be the goalie, allow a peer to assist. Do not allow the student with a shunt to play the goalie position.
- For soccer outdoors, provide sideline activities for the student in the wheelchair and allow a peer to interact with the student until it is his or her turn to participate. Peers may switch in and out at this point.
- Only the paraeducator should push the student in the wheelchair when this is needed.

Volleyball

- Allow the student in the wheelchair to catch the ball and throw it back over the net.
- Use a lower net if needed.
- Use a softer ball (e.g., a beach ball).
- Allow the ball to bounce before the student attempts to catch it.
- Provide assistance from the paraprofessional or another student if needed.
- Allow the paraeducator or the peer to catch the ball for the student in the wheelchair.

▶ Wheelchair hockey modification.

- If the student has no upper body strength or control, the para-educator or peer will need to assist in returning the ball over the net. This can be done with a volley or a throw.

Hockey

- Use a shorter stick for the student in the wheelchair, as well as a larger ball to dribble.
- For some students you may need to actually tape a stick to the chair so that the student can push him- or herself or be pushed by the paraeducator.
- Tether a ball to the student's chair and allow the student to pull the ball back if possible after striking it during drills.

Ping Pong

- Use balloons and paddles for a student who has a difficult time tracking the ball or who has delayed motor responses.
- If the student in the wheelchair has no upper body strength or control, use a bolster and have the student sit on a mat. The para-educator will need to assist by helping the student stay upright and will need to choose a peer to interact with the student and volley the balloon back and forth. This will help the student develop trunk control.

- If the student is able to hold the paddle in a fixed position, a peer or the paraeducator can hit the ball so that it rebounds off the paddle and returns to them. This usually works best on a regular table with a net or make shift net.
- Some students in wheelchairs who are able to sit on the floor enjoy playing ping pong on the floor with a partner. This works best in a station or as a sideline activity.

Pinball Games

- Though dodgeball and bombardment games have fallen out of favor with most physical educators, some still allow the students to play games in which teams attempt to knock down pins of opposing teams. For these games, set up a safety zone for the student in a wheelchair. No other students are allowed in this safety zone (unless you choose to use another student to deflect stray balls), nor are others allowed to throw balls in this area. However, a peer or the paraeducator will need to retrieve balls for the student to throw at the opposing team's pins.
- If the student is unable to throw balls, place a bowling pin or target in an area for the student to roll the ball at during the game. Use a bowling ramp if needed.

Kickball or Baseball

- Use tape to outline extra bases (create extra-large bases next to the regular bases that chairs can roll over). The students without disabilities use the regular bases, and the students in wheelchairs use the tape bases.
- Use a shorter distance between bases for the student in the wheelchair by placing the tape bases such that the tape base path is half the length of the regular base path.
- Allow the student in the wheelchair to throw the ball out into the field instead of kicking it.
- If the student is really flexible, he or she may be able to lean over and strike the kickball with a hand.
- Place the ball on a cone or a tee for the student to strike.
- Provide a bowling ramp for the student to use to roll the ball into the field.
- Never allow other students to hit the student in a wheelchair with a ball.
- Once the student in the wheelchair strikes, hits, or rolls the ball into the field, instruct the fielders to count to 10 out loud before retrieving the ball.

- Have the paraeducator push the student in the wheelchair for running the bases. As I suggested earlier, it would not be appropriate for the peer facilitator to push the student in the wheelchair during a game.

Tumbling

- Students in wheelchairs may be able to get out of their chairs for tumbling activities if they do not have a medical condition that will restrict them (such as a shunt) and if they can support themselves with their upper bodies.
- Provide a separate mat for the student who can get out of the wheelchair and allow a peer or two to join the student. Inform these peers of safety rules for the student.
- Assist in the log roll by physically rolling the student, and give the student a lightweight implement such as a noodle or plastic bat to hold in his or her hand to knock a pin over at the end of the mat or along the side of the mat.
- Do not allow forward rolls, backward rolls, or egg rolls, which could put pressure on the student's neck.
- Substitute tumbling rolls or animal walks for stunts that the student cannot perform.
- Use a bolster to aid the student in maintaining posture during sitting.
- Have the student lie stomach down on the mat and pull him- or herself across the mat while holding on to a dowel held by the teacher or paraeducator.
- If the student cannot get out of the chair, this would be a good time to present a parallel activity on the sidelines. For example, with parallel tumbling activities, place a folded tumbling mat on two scooters; use a gait belt or Velcro strap to secure the student on the mat. If possible, have the student hold a rope, and pull the student alongside the tumbling area or around the available free space in the gym. Or, using the same setup, have the student hold a bat or noodle and attempt to knock pins down while being pushed or pulled about.

Obstacle Courses

- Set up an extra, shortened obstacle course for the student in a wheelchair that parallels the course for the able-bodied students.
- Use lots of unders and weaving through cones or ropes on the floor.

- Design a course for the student using tape on the floor. The student can follow the trail.
- Add objects for the student to retrieve and place in a container.
- Use a timer if the student needs more competition.

Relays

- When teaching relays, keep the student in the wheelchair in an outside lane and adapt for dribbling, catching, and so on.
- For dribbling, the student holds the ball in the lap and pushes the chair or is pushed by the paraeducator if he or she is unable to maneuver the wheelchair. Some students will actually be able to dribble the ball a few times.
- For catching, use tethered balls or allow another student to retrieve fumbled balls.
- This would also be a good time to use a rope (or hoop) for the student to hold on to, in order to be pulled by the teacher or paraeducator, if the student has a low level of upper body strength.
- For jumping rope, push the student in the chair and allow the student to swing or twirl the rope on one side of his or her body.
- For scooter relays, if possible, allow the younger students to sit in your lap and help them perform the relay in a safe manner. Or, hook two scooters together, place a mat on top and use the student's gait belt to secure him or her to the mat and push or pull the student with a rope.

Rhythms

- Use ribbons or streamers for the student in the wheelchair when teaching rhythms.
- Some students will be able to move their chairs to the beat of the music by rolling the wheels back and forth. Others may need the paraeducator to do this.

Parachute

- Parachute activities are great for students in wheelchairs. Allow them to hold on to the parachute if possible, but monitor. Do not allow them to put a hand through the handles.
- Assist the student in the wheelchair when he or she is going under the parachute; you may need to lift the parachute to keep the student from rolling over the material.

Stations or Centers

- Stations or centers are also great for students in wheelchairs because they can involve peer helpers, which will benefit both students.

- For tossing and catching, students can use boxes or scoops to catch balls or beanbags thrown to them.

- Teach the peer student to bounce a ball into the lap of the student in the wheelchair.

- If using jump ropes, allow the student in the wheelchair to twirl the long rope for other jumpers; if the student cannot twirl, tie the rope to the chair.

- Provide extra activities in the centers that students in wheel-chairs will be capable of performing. For example, a student may be good at rolling balls at targets instead of throwing balls at the targets.

- Provide a bowling ramp that the student with no upper body strength can use to roll the ball at targets or to a partner.

Fitness Testing

- For fitness testing, have the student in a wheelchair use a 2-foot (0.6-meter) dowel to do pull-ups. The teacher or paraeducator will need to hold the dowel above the student's head and allow the student to pull up until rising from the wheelchair about an inch or two.

- Students may also do wheelchair push-ups. They must first lock the brakes on the wheelchair and then remove the waist strap. Then they place their hands on the arms of the chair and push their body up until their bottom leaves the chair. They hold the position for 5 to 10 seconds and gradually increase the time and number of repetitions.

▶ A student performing a wheelchair push-up for a fitness test.

- Allow a student who can get out of the wheelchair to lie on a mat on his or her back and pull up on the bar or dowel as you hold it.

- Shorten the distance of the shuttle run and allow a peer to hand the student in the wheelchair the object to retrieve.

- For the sit and reach, hold a ruler for the student and allow the student to reach forward while still sitting in the chair. Or, allow the student to actually reach with a ruler in his or her hand when using the sit and reach box.

- Shorten the distance of the mile run. Allow the students to push themselves around the gym a comfortable distance based on each individual's abilities.

- Push the students in wheelchairs who cannot maneuver their chairs for the mile run. Again, shorten the distance.

PARALLEL ACTIVITIES FOR STUDENTS WITH UPPER BODY CONTROL

If the student in the wheelchair is unable to participate in the planned activity for safety reasons or lack of proper supervision, use parallel activities on the sidelines based on the student's ability levels. Even students who require a paraeducator for support in order to become successful benefit from peer helpers in these parallel activities. They feel more included when doing the parallel activities on the sidelines with a peer. In my experience, especially in the elementary schools, peers are usually eager to assist students in wheelchairs. They are very intrigued by the wheelchair and often have to be reminded to give the student room to maneuver.

Always encourage students with disabilities to participate and to make suggestions for how they can participate safely in physical activities. This is simple to do and provides direction for you as the teacher, as well as giving the student self-confidence. The student develops decision-making skills and learns to be his or her own advocate.

If you can, choose sideline activities that are related to the activity the general students are doing. The following ideas can get you started.

- Students in wheelchairs can push a ball out of their lap in an attempt to knock down pins.

- They can use a bowling ramp to knock pins down, to aim at other targets, or to play catch with a peer.

▶ The student is out of his chair, developing upper body strength by pulling on a rope held by a peer.

- They can catch balls or beanbags thrown by a partner using a milk jug scoop or small fishing net or a box on the lap.
- Tie a rope to a door handle, the bleachers, a goal, or a sturdy object and have students pull themselves in their chairs to the object (this is obviously for students with good upper body strength).
- Have students toss beanbags at targets.
- Tether a wiffle ball to the chair and have the student throw the ball at a target and then pull the ball back.
- Have students practice driving their electric or manual chair through cones.
- Have them shoot baskets at a lower goal or a makeshift goal (trash can, box, or basket).
- Have them throw the soccer ball at a goalie set up on the sideline.
- Have them volley balloons or a beach ball back and forth with a partner.
- Students can shoot at a goal (made with two cones) with a hockey stick and a large ball; in some cases this may even be hand over hand.

- They can hit a ball off a tee or cone; add pins to knock down to make this more exciting (have students use a bat, racket, or paddle for striking).

MODIFICATIONS FOR STUDENTS WITH LIMITED OR NO UPPER BODY CONTROL

The student with limited or no upper body control will need much more hands-on assistance than the student possessing more control, and may often need to participate in parallel activities. The paraeducator or peer facilitator or both are key in assisting the student to participate and feel successful. The paraeducator should push the nonmobile student in the wheelchair, but can actually teach the peer facilitator to use the hand-over-hand technique by fading assistance and observing from a close distance in case there is a need to intercede.

The same rules apply for tag games as for the student with upper body control. Tags can be accumulated, and any balls thrown as a tag in a dodgeball-type game should be rolled at the back wheels of the chair. In addition, general students can be asked to deflect balls rolled at the student's chair, or safety zones can be set up to protect the student from thrown balls. Never allow balls to be thrown, kicked, or batted at a student in a wheelchair who cannot use the upper body to protect him- or herself. As already noted, these students may be medically fragile or may have a shunt that could be damaged, with serious or life-threatening consequences.

PARALLEL ACTIVITIES FOR STUDENTS WITH LIMITED OR NO UPPER BODY CONTROL

Hand-over-hand techniques will be required to assist the student with limited or no upper body strength or control. In this technique, the paraeducator assists the student by actually holding the equipment with the student. For example, the paraeducator helps the student swing the bat or throw a beanbag. In rare cases, if the student is too stiff or too fragile to grasp equipment, the paraeducator will need to hold the bat or racket next to the student to allow performance of the skill.

Even if students have no upper body strength or control and require a paraeducator, they still benefit from peer facilitators. The following suggested activities are designed for use with peer facilitators and allow the peers to participate as well as assist.

Hand-Over-Hand Activities

- Using a bat or racket to hit balls thrown from a peer
- Using a noodle to hit balloons thrown from a peer
- Throwing Frisbees at bowling pins
- Hitting a ball off a tee in an attempt to knock down pins
- Hitting with a hockey stick in an attempt to score on a goalie
- Driving the chair in an attempt to dribble a ball (use a large ball) with a hockey stick that is tied or taped to the wheelchair
- Using a box to catch beanbags, sponge balls, or wiffle balls thrown by the peer

MODIFIED GAMES
FOR STUDENTS WITH LIMITED
OR NO UPPER BODY CONTROL

These activities can be used as sideline activities or in centers with the general class. All students will enjoy the activities, and it will be easy to include the students in wheelchairs. Very few modifications are needed for these activities to incorporate all learners. However, the paraeducator's assistance will be crucial if these activities are used as sideline activities and in some situations when they are used in centers or stations.

ROLLING TARGETS

Tape a box or a crate onto a scooter. Tie the scooter to the student's wheelchair. Have the peer facilitators form two parallel lines approximately 15 to 20 feet (4.6 to 6 meters) apart. The peers will be in a sitting position and will attempt to throw beanbags into the rolling target tied to the student's chair. The student in the wheelchair will drive the wheelchair through the parallel lines. Play continues until all beanbags are in the box.

Inclusion for the general class: This game can also be played with the general class rather than as a parallel activity, and general peers can take turns pulling the box tied to a scooter. Or, the general peers can push the box through the lane area as others attempt to toss the beanbags into the box.

FLAG TAG

Place football flag tags all over the student's chair and have peer facilitators sit on scooters with flags attached to their waist or around their shoulders. Choose one person to be "it." The "it" person will attempt to pull the flags from all players. Once a student's flag has been pulled, he or she will then become "it" along with the original "it." Play stops when all players are without flags, including the original "it."

Inclusion for the general class: This game can also be played in the same manner with the whole class. If you do not have enough scooters for all the students, play the game in timed intervals. You will have to be creative about placement of flags for the students on the scooters. If you have flag belts, place them over one shoulder and under the other arm.

CONE COMBINATIONS

Have different-colored cones scattered throughout the playing area, with a beanbag balancing on top of each cone. Instruct the student in a chair to drive (or be pushed) to the cones in certain color combinations (e.g., red first, then green, then yellow), and time the student to see how long it takes for him or her to knock all beanbags off the cones. If you do not have multicolored cones, don't worry about the sequencing of the cones. Allow the peer facilitators to attempt the same activity on scooters. The students are competing against themselves, not each other.

Inclusion for the general class: This could also be used as a relay for the whole class. Place a beanbag on only one cone. Have all students scoot down in turn; one student knocks the beanbag off the cone and the next student in line places the bag back on the cone.

RACING FOR POINTS

Place spot markers 6 to 10 feet (2 to 3 meters) apart with numbered points of 10, 20, 30, and so on. Inform the student that he or she has 10 to 15 seconds to score as many points as possible by driving to each spot. Allow the peer facilitators to do the same with scooters.

Inclusion for the general class: Do this activity in a station or center.

RACING RIBBONS

Make a finish line with string and streamers and tie it to a door or standards about 15 to 20 yards from the start. On the "go" signal, have the student in the wheelchair race the peer facilitators who are on scooters or who are doing a type of animal walk (crab, bear, duck, horse [gallop], and so on). They enjoy the streamers as they pass through the finish line.

Inclusion for the general class: Provide the activity for the general class either with scooters or as a running event.

SPEED SOCCER GOALIE

Set up a soccer goal with two large cones at a distance of 6 to 8 feet (2 to 2.4 meters). Have the student in the wheelchair position him- or herself at one cone. On a signal, have a peer kick with the nondominant foot in an attempt to score. The student in the wheelchair will time his or her drive so as to stop the ball. If needed, have a peer facilitator assist as goalie by following the student in the wheelchair to deflect balls that rise above the level of the chair wheels. Do not use this game with a student in a wheelchair who has a shunt.

Inclusion for the general class: Use this activity as a drill for soccer. Have the paraeducator monitor the drill, especially since the students will be kicking with the nondominant foot.

CONCLUSION

Students in wheelchairs add a new dimension to your class; with a little creative thinking and planning, physical education can be a successful and fun learning environment for them. In every class I've had that included a student in a wheelchair, he or she has been accepted and admired by the general students. Within the context of all the disabilities, general students really understand that students in wheelchairs have to work a little harder to get things done and respect any ability that the student in a wheelchair has. They truly want the student to succeed, and many of them want to help make that happen.

chapter 4

Including Students With Intellectual Disabilities

Working with individuals who have intellectual disabilities (ID) has been one of the most rewarding experiences in my teaching career. Students with ID love attention from others and are very caring and giving toward others. They respond well to praise and encouragement and give lots of smiles and hugs in return. Their kindness and love are very genuine and come straight from their hearts. Given the chance, they will touch you and your students deeply.

Students with ID have developmental delays and a below-normal IQ, and they learn at a slower rate than their typical peers. Some of the common forms of ID that you may see in your classes are Down syndrome, Fragile X syndrome, Williams syndrome, and traumatic brain injury (TBI), to name a few. Other forms of ID are caused by congenital infections, environmental factors, or even prenatal exposure to alcohol or drugs. Often, and in addition, some children with ID have physical disabilities in conjunction with their cognitive or developmental delays (Krebs, 2005).

Students with ID have attention difficulties and struggle to stay focused. Because of memory problems they have difficulty storing and retrieving information. They have difficulty in simple problem solving and generalizing. It is difficult for them to apply something already learned to a new situation because of a limited ability to think abstractly. As more concrete thinkers, they are bound to the immediate situation, and it is easier for them to understand something that they have seen or touched (Gioia, 1993).

Basically, students with developmental or intellectual disabilities have to "learn how to learn." For this reason, in physical education it is important to break skills down into small increments and teach these skills systematically. For example, it is important that students with ID obtain certain basic skills such as kicking a stationary ball before they can be taught more advanced skills such as kicking a rolled ball or kicking at a target. Teaching progression in skill development is essential for their success.

Children with ID also learn social skills at a slower rate than others (Gioia, 1993). Most children with disabilities have a limited number of play experiences, which increases this deficit in social interaction. Therefore, any opportunity to interact with their general peers is to their advantage. In addition, interacting with others motivates students with ID to try new things and teaches them to follow the rules in order to be a part of a group.

Another way children with ID may differ from others is in their motor planning. For example, they can be delayed in how their brain plans when and how to move; how to decide which limbs move first,

▶ Students with ID can learn valuable social skills through interaction with their non-disabled peers.

second, and third; and how to position their body (Gioia, 1993). Their brains work hard to perform motor tasks, and this drains their ability to attend. For this reason, they sometimes need extra time to respond to a command or just to perform a basic skill. In addition, they often have problems with balance and strength, which affect fine motor skills and even their posture or ability to sit. These issues need to be addressed with extra patience and individual support.

Most states or districts classify students with ID into four categories: *mild, moderate, severe,* and *profound.* In the state of Georgia, students with mild ID are labeled MID and can often acquire academic skills up to a sixth grade level. Students classified as moderately intellectually disabled (MOID) have an overall mental age of 5 to 8 years. As a combined group, students with severe or profound intellectual disabilities (SID/PID) require high levels of structure and supervision and may or may not have communication skills (Boyles & Contadino, 1998). In general, the more severe the ID, the slower the development of the student will be in comparison to the general population. You can find out more about your state's classification system from the administration in your school or from the special education department in your school system.

It is important to collaborate with the special education teacher or paraeducator of these students to identify any restrictions or medical issues. These issues could include heart disease, respiratory problems, seizures, behavioral problems, attention deficit disorder (ADD) or attention deficit hyperactivity disorder (ADHD), or communication and speech problems. However, with a strong support system, individuals with ID can benefit from inclusive learning environments and have successful experiences.

Students with ID are more like nondisabled students than they are different from them. They love to be around people, especially their peers; they love to be the center of attention; and they love to play. They need guidance in these areas but definitely respond to and need these interactions. Understanding this is the first step to including students with ID in your classroom successfully.

BENEFITS OF INCLUSION FOR STUDENTS WITH INTELLECTUAL DISABILITIES

As discussed in chapter 1, the law requires that special education students attend school in the *least restrictive environment* (LRE), and this means in a setting that permits maximum contact with normally developing children (Boyles & Contadino, 1998). Inclusion can come in many different packages and according to research has proven to be very effective and beneficial for learners with ID.

When we consider the areas of cognitive, social, and motor development, the importance of integrating physical education in the curriculum is obvious for students with ID. Inclusion in physical education helps develop an intrinsic desire to play for students who are intellectually disabled, especially those who lack the opportunity to participate in social situations. Without social skills it is hard for them to learn motivation and self-discipline. The more fun they have, the more motivated they are and the more desire they have to participate. According to experts, play is one of the most important means that a child with ID has to interact with others and to grow as an individual (Morris & Schulz, 1989).

That said, play is not always easy for the child with an ID. The child must initially learn to play as an individual and figure out how to use body parts such as the feet and hands, as well as equipment for object control and manipulation. Next, the child must learn to play near others and eventually interact with others during play. Later the child can learn to play games that require sharing, group cooperation, and taking turns. Most importantly, play should be fun in order to motivate the student so that play can be internalized (Morris & Schulz, 1989).

Inclusion in the general environment will require essential support from a paraeducator or peer facilitator for students with MOID or SID/PID. In my experience, students with MID may or may not need support. They usually need modifications in the delivery of the instructions, which need to be concrete and simple. And, for those students having a difficult time understanding the instructions or rules, simply providing a peer facilitator will take care of the circumstance. However, some students who are MID may be shy and reserved and could melt away unnoticed if support is not provided. In addition, behavioral issues could arise for the student who feels intimidated or confused. Again collaboration with the student's teacher will help you determine the support needed for your students with ID.

The following are some general tips for including students with ID in your classroom.

- Be patient and remember that the students have delays that will hinder understanding, progression, and success.
- Be flexible; know that the students will sometimes break the rules because they don't understand them, so reiterate or use simpler cues.
- Have peers make up rules that others can understand and that are fair for everyone.
- Recognize that you can make a difference in the student's experience.
- Have a positive attitude toward inclusion, and include the peer facilitators and paraeducators in the process.
- Find the students' strengths and develop those strengths. Understand that they have abilities too.
- Provide lots of positive reinforcements and feedback; high fives and words of encouragement go a long way for students who are not motivated to participate, and most need specific individual praise.
- Use concrete boundaries such as spot markers (poly spots), ropes, or cones for games, skills, or drills. The student can be referred to the spot when confused or out of control.
- Modify the equipment so that it is less intimidating or easier to use; examples are lighter balls and rackets.
- Modify rules based on the learner's level of comprehension. Sometimes just removing a rule will provide the most effective

modification. For example, alter rules that the student cannot understand, or allow the student to take extra steps when dribbling a basketball or to acquire extra tags in a game of chase.

- Break tasks into smaller steps to keep students from becoming overwhelmed. This will minimize frustrations.
- When breaking tasks into smaller steps, demonstrate the steps; many students with ID are visual learners.
- Use basic concrete and simple cues, as well as visual demonstrations, to compensate for the student's inability to remember and think abstractly. Ask them to repeat key parts of the directions.
- Allow varying levels of participation. Eventually, these levels increase with the student's comfort level.
- Understand that waiting in line for a turn is difficult for some students. Avoid games with lots of waiting in line or allow the student to perform another task, such as dribbling or throwing a ball with a peer, while waiting.
- Plan multiple activities, especially for younger students, to compensate for their short attention spans.
- Don't get frustrated when students fail; as long as they are having fun, encourage them to continue trying.
- Look for small achievements over time—you will see gradual improvements.
- Use a consistent routine: warm-ups, activity or game, closing.
- Expect students to participate, expect them to be nice to others, and expect them to listen when you are talking. Be consistent in your expectations.
- Celebrate the process, not just the product.
- Understand that students with ID are a lot like their general peers and need as many as possible of the same experiences that are provided to the general peers.

The following rating scales (tables 4.1 and 4.2) are samples that I developed for my students in adapted physical education. The scales show the progression for my students' skills in social and motor development. These scales can serve as guidelines for physical educators concerning social and motor development for all students, but especially those with exceptionalities and cognitive delays.

Table 4.1

RATING SCALE FOR MOTOR SKILLS

STUDENT: _____

CRITERIA	1 INITIAL	2 EMERGING	3 PROGRESSING	4 FUNCTIONAL	SCORE × 25
Running	Needs prompts	Runs randomly	Follows course or direction; follows course through obstacles	Evades field of stationary objects; evades field of moving objects and others	
Kicking	Kicks with prompts; kicks with assistance	Kicks stationary ball	Kicks rolled ball	Kicks with moving or rapid approach	
Striking	Strikes with prompts; strikes with assistance	Strikes tethered ball; strikes ball off tee	Strikes rolled ball	Strikes a pitched ball	
Catching	Catches with assistance; catches tethered ball	Catches rolled ball	Catches slowly tossed ball to midline	Moves to catch ball	
Throwing	Throws with prompts; throws with assistance	Throws forward to stationary target or individual	Throws to slowly moving target	Throws to target moving randomly in area	
Jumping	Jumps with prompts; jumps with assistance	Jumps forward	Jumps forward varying distances	Jumps down from height; jumps up to height	
Galloping	Runs with uneven rhythm	Moves forward using same lead foot and trunk sideways	Moves forward using same lead foot and trunk forward	Gallops with consistent rhythm	
Hopping	One-foot to two-foot landing	Hops up and down with support	Hops up and down; hops forward	Hops down from height; hops up to height	
Skipping	Runs, gallops, or leaps	Same-side skip	Segmented alternate skip, irregular rhythm	Skips with consistent pattern; skips rhythmically	
Dribbling	Dribbles with assistance	Bounces and catches	Dribbles continuously using same hand	Dribbles continuously using alternate hand	

Adapted, by permission, from S. Kasser, 1995, *Inclusive Games* (Champaign, IL: Human Kinetics), 13.

Table 4.2

RATING SCALE FOR SOCIAL DEVELOPMENT

STUDENT: _____

CRITERIA	1 INITIAL	2 EMERGING	3 PROGRESSING	4 FUNCTIONAL	SCORE × 25
Socialization	Needs prompts to interact with others	Interacts with teacher with no prompts	Interacts with peers with no prompts	Interacts with group	
Cooperation	Follows rules with prompts	Takes turns	Shares equipment and space with others	Initiates interaction with others	
Understanding fitness goals	Needs prompts to participate	Chooses to participate in activities	Works independently with minimal assistance to pursue fitness	Identifies principles of practice and conditioning	
Following rules	Needs prompts	Understands minimal amounts	Begins to show consistency	Understands cause and effect of game situations	

Developed by Pattie Rouse, Cherokee County Schools, October 2008. Based on the Georgia Performance Standards.

GAMES AND ACTIVITIES FOR ALL ABILITIES

Simple games that are oriented toward success motivate students with ID to participate with others. In addition, such games help to develop and maintain many valuable skills that enhance the student's everyday life:

- **Socialization.** The students learn how to take turns and to cooperate with others. They learn respect for themselves and others. In addition, they learn self-discipline while having fun.
- **Speech and language skills.** Having the opportunity to interact with others develops much needed speech and language skills for the student with ID. The student learns to communicate by responding to verbal prompts from a peer or teacher and eventually initiates conversation when needing help. In addition, the student may initiate conversation just from the sheer joy of having fun through play.

- **Motor planning.** Playing games over and over will help students learn specific steps that will increase their ability to motor plan and develop certain skills. For example, the student who is having difficulty releasing the ball when attempting to throw at a target or an opponent can practice the skill of throwing during the game and can be given individualized help if needed. I have noticed that if I count to three, the student with motor delays will often attempt the skill that I am asking him to perform. I have also noticed when providing repetition of these basic skills, some of my students' delays improve. According to experts, improving motor skills also improves language disorders.

- **Sequencing events.** Learning to follow directions will improve the student's ability to sequence events through following steps that will provide the cause and effect of the game. For example, the cause includes step 1 (pick up the ball) and step 2 (roll the ball at the opponent), and the effect is the outcome of the opponent's being tagged with the ball. Begin with games with simple directions. Have the student repeat the directions and then carry them out in the correct sequence.

- **Memory enhancement.** Learning to play games can enhance memory and recall, which are very difficult for many students with ID. The teacher often needs to stop and review the rules or ask the students to verbalize the next step in the process in order for this to happen. Games provide short tasks that the student can complete quickly and successfully, which over time will enhance his or her ability to remember the rules.

The following games and activities, which are not highly structured, are designed to promote fun and fitness. For the most part, the games and activities are nonelimination, with little emphasis on winning, and some are continuous in play. The main goals are to provide opportunities for the students to have fun while cooperating with others in an effort to learn to share, take turns, and develop basic motor skills. The key is participation, not competition.

These games are appropriate for students of all exceptionalities, including groups in a general physical education classroom. The variations described will help you to use the games in a self-contained or general physical education environment and to make the games more challenging or less difficult for groups with lower functioning students. Adaptations are included to provide the opportunities for students of all abilities to participate whether they have a physical or a cognitive delay.

In addition, the drills and activities at the end of the chapter will provide opportunities for your students to develop motor skills through repetition and practice. If used in the general physical education classroom, most of the drills will work well in centers or stations. They also present opportunities for general peers to assist students with different exceptionalities.

A main concern related to teaching students with cognitive delays is whether to teach games and activities that are age appropriate based on chronological age, or to teach games and activities based on cognitive or developmental ability. Since you know your students best, decide which games and activities are appropriate for your students. I have found that age appropriateness is not as much about the skill that is being taught as about how the activity is presented. For example, I would not use a stuffed animal as a piece of equipment to teach skills to my high school students with third grade skill levels, but I would teach them these same skills with more age-appropriate equipment. However, you will also find that some of these games and activities actually take into consideration both developmental and chronological age.

HEAD START

PLAYERS
Any number and all levels

AREA
Gym or outdoor area

SKILLS
Fitness, following directions

EQUIPMENT
Cones for markers if outside area is used

ACTIVITY
Instruct all students to line up in a horizontal line across the baseline of the gym floor. Choose or ask a volunteer to stand on the free throw line or on one of the blocks around the lane. This will be the student with the "head start." On the "go" signal, all students race to the opposite baseline. Hopefully, but not always, the head-start student will arrive first. Praise and give the student a high five whether he or she arrives first or not. Then choose another head-start person.

VARIATIONS
- Adjust the head-start position according to the student's ability level.
- Choose more than one head-start person. This will also motivate others and help them feel less intimidated.
- Set the game up with partners; the students would be competing with only one person.
- You can choose to allow the students to tag the head-start person if you think it is appropriate. You will need to explain the "tag" versus a "push."

- This game would work well in a general physical education setting if you use more head-start players or partners.

ADAPTATIONS

- Physically prompt or guide the student who appears less motivated or who just needs the prompt to get started because of motor delays.
- Use a tether or a sighted guide for the student who is blind.
- Push a student in a wheelchair who needs the assistance.
- Assist the student with severe delays at all times.

TEACHING NOTES

My students love this activity, though some do need to be motivated. With my smaller groups I use one head-start person, and with larger groups I use three or more. I also use this as an opening or closing activity. I use it with elementary through high school students who have cognitive delays.

RETRIEVAL

PLAYERS

Large or small groups for all grade levels

AREA

Gym, hallway, outdoor area

SKILLS

Agility, fitness, cooperation

EQUIPMENT

Two wiffle balls or small Gator Skin balls; a box, crate, or bucket

ACTIVITY

Instruct the students to form two parallel lines behind a starting line, each in the same position in the line as the person that he or she would like to race. Inform the participants that they will each run to retrieve one of the two balls you will throw out. Once retrieving the balls, the two students will race back to the starting line in an attempt to drop their ball into the box before their opponent does. As you toss the balls forward you should adjust the distance according to the retrievers' abilities and give a "go" signal. The distance will range from 10 feet (3 meters) to 20 or 30 yards (18 or 27 meters). Students then return to the back of the line and choose the next person that they would like to race.

VARIATIONS

- Roll the balls instead of throwing.
- Increase or decrease the distance thrown.
- Use a smaller box or bucket for placing the balls with more accuracy.

ADAPTATIONS

- Retrieve the ball for the student in a wheelchair and assist in mobility if necessary.

- Assist the student who has visual impairment with mobility and with retrieving the ball.
- Assist the student with more severe ID; this may involve leading the student or retrieving the ball and having the student place the ball in the box.

TEACHING NOTES

This is a great closing activity for any class. Avoid emphasis on winners and losers for students with cognitive delays by keeping the game fast paced with lots of throws. All grade and ability levels enjoy this game.

FOLLOW THE FUN

PLAYERS

Small or large groups of elementary level or higher; modify equipment for students with lower skill levels and use age-appropriate equipment for students with higher skill levels.

AREA

Gym or hard-surface outdoor area

SKILLS

Following directions, object control, locomotor skills, and fitness

EQUIPMENT

Playground ball per student, 10 or more bowling pins

ACTIVITY

Spread the pins across the baseline of the gym and instruct all students to line up on the midcourt line facing the pins, with a ball in their hands. Then give the students a verbal directive about a skill to perform at the midcourt line and about how to travel with the ball to the pins. When arriving near the pins, the students are allowed to roll or throw the ball in an attempt to knock the pins down. When all pins are down, have students reset them and then run back to the midline, and start with another directive.

Examples of directives for students to follow after a "go" signal:

- Drop and catch the ball at midcourt, then run to the pins.
- Toss and catch the ball at midcourt, then skip to the pins.
- Lean over, then roll and tap the ball to the pins.
- Dribble two times, then slide to the pins.
- Toss, clap, and catch, then gallop to the pins.

VARIATIONS

- To motivate students, have them keep score as a group.
- This activity could be used in a general physical education classroom with two large groups and pins on each baseline. The two groups could compete (score goes to group that gets all pins down first).

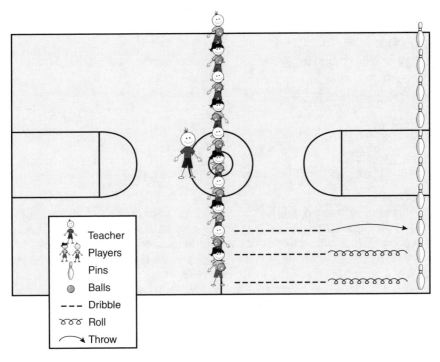

▶ Follow the Fun.

ADAPTATIONS
- Decrease or increase skills according to students' ability levels.
- Use a tethered ball for a student in a wheelchair.
- Push students in wheelchairs who cannot push themselves, with the ball in their lap.
- Use a tethered rope to lead the student who is blind, or use a tethered ball and verbally guide the student or use a sighted guide with elbow lead if possible.
- Assist the student with severe cognitive delays at all times. For example, you may need to actually dribble, toss, or catch for the student or use hand-over-hand instruction.
- Use a physical versus a verbal "go" signal for the student who is hearing impaired.

TEACHING NOTES
I use this activity for students who need to practice following directions and who need specific skill development. They enjoy the freedom of working independently in this activity. They love to reset the pins. I use this activity mostly with elementary-level groups that are MID or MOID.

SCOOTER BOWLING

PLAYERS
Large or small group for elementary or middle school level

AREA
Gym, hallway, or classroom

SKILLS
Cooperation and strength

EQUIPMENT
Scooters (one per partnership if possible), bowling pins

ACTIVITY
Set up area with two parallel boundary lines approximately 10 to 15 yards (9 to 14 meters) apart; along a line in the center, place bowling pins, one for each set of partners. Divide the students into partners of equal size and ability. One partner sits on the scooter, and the other partner gives that person a push toward their pin in an attempt to knock it over. If they miss, they continue until the pin is knocked over. Once the pin is down and the student on the scooter reaches the other boundary, the partners exchange positions and continue to attempt to knock the pin over (The students can reset the pin or the teacher or paraeducator can reset it.). It is important to instruct the student on the scooter to stiffen the upper body and to instruct the pusher to place his or her hands on the person's shoulder blades before pushing.

Sometimes I set this game up for my elementary self-contained classes with a teacher on each boundary; the student is pushed from each side before returning to the back of the line. In this instance, there will be at least four students on a scooter waiting to be pushed. This is more work for the teachers, but the students have a blast!

VARIATIONS
- The teacher pushes the students on the scooters.
- The student on the scooter holds a rope that is pulled by the partner.

ADAPTATIONS
- Allow the student in a wheelchair to sit or lie on a doubled scooter with a mat on top. You may need to use a Velcro belt to secure the student. **Only the teacher or paraeducator** pushes the student, and **the student must not be shoved.**
- Use a tethered rope for pulling the student with visual impairment.
- Assist the SID student; this may even mean that you sit on the scooter and allow the student to sit in your lap. I have done this with my students with SID and cerebral palsy who are unable to bend their bodies to sit on the scooter.

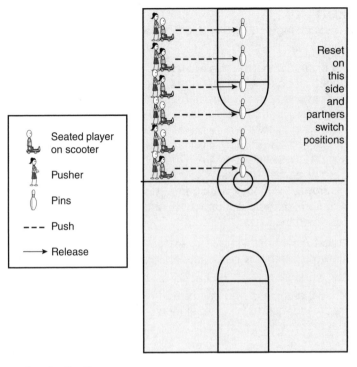

Reset on this side and partners switch positions

Seated player on scooter

Pusher

Pins

--- Push

⟶ Release

▶ Scooter Bowling.

TEACHING NOTES

This game is appropriate for any self-contained classroom as the activity for the day. However, for students in general physical education, the activity is recommended for stations or relays. Or the game can be used as a parallel activity for students unable to participate in the regular activity in the general classroom. My students with cognitive delays in all grades and with all ability levels enjoy this game. The MID and MOID students also enjoy pushing other students on the scooters.

CABOOSE

PLAYERS
Large or small group for elementary and some middle school students

AREA
Gym or open area with hard floors (such as open hallways)

SKILLS
Fitness, throwing (at a moving target)

EQUIPMENT

Scooter with box taped on top and lots of beanbags

ACTIVITY

Tape a box or crate about the size of a large scooter, or a bit larger, to a scooter. Give each student as many beanbags as he or she can handle (this number will range from one to five). Instruct the students that you will be pushing the scooter (caboose) around the gym area and they will be chasing the caboose and attempting to throw the beanbags into the caboose. If the students miss hitting the moving target, they are instructed to pick the beanbags up and continue throwing until all bags are in the caboose. Rest time is often needed throughout the game. The faster you push the caboose and the more you dodge the crowd, the more fun the game seems to be. With this in mind, make sure that the box or crate is sturdy enough to take the weight of your hands bearing down on the sides.

VARIATIONS

- Adjust the number of beanbags according to each student's abilities.
- Allow students to push the caboose.
- For a general class, you can have the students push the caboose in a lane area formed by all other students sitting on parallel lines.

▶ Caboose.

ADAPTATIONS

- Use parallel boundary lines as a start and a finish for students with more involved impairments.
- Stop the caboose for students who have a difficult time keeping a faster pace and allow them to throw at a stationary caboose target.
- Use peer helpers or paraeducators for students in wheelchairs who are nonmobile.
- Tie the caboose to the chair of the student who drives an electric chair.
- Allow students with SID who are unable to chase the caboose to sit inside the box, and have the other students attempt to tag the box instead of throwing items into the box. However, know that if you do this, others will expect to ride in the box. I use this as a closing activity for some of my self-contained classes, and they love it!

TEACHING NOTES

This game is so much fun that the students can't help participating. My high school students with ID enjoy this game as much as my elementary students. Each time we play it, I am shocked at the students who volunteer to push the caboose; even my hard-to-motivate students love this game and choose to be "it" or to push the caboose. This game is easy to incorporate into a general physical education class with few modifications. I would start with dividing the entire group into smaller groups if it includes two or more classes. You can also assign more than one caboose.

PARTNER LINE-KICKBALL

PLAYERS

Small or large group for elementary level and higher levels with modifications

AREA

Gym or outdoor surface

SKILLS

Kicking skills, cooperation, sharing

EQUIPMENT

Poly spots, balls, bowling pins

ACTIVITY

Place poly spots in two parallel lines approximately 30 or 40 feet (9 or 12 meters) apart, one poly spot for each student. Place a group of bowling pins for each pair of partners in a horizontal line between the two lines of poly spots. Divide the group into partners and have the partners stand on opposite sides on the poly spots facing each other. Play starts on the "go" signal. One partner kicks the ball in an attempt to knock down the pins in the middle. The other partner will retrieve the ball and kick it back from his or her poly spot, also in an attempt to knock the pins down. All players continue kicking until all pins are down. Then, reset and continue play.

The paraeducator or teacher may need to remind partners to retrieve the ball when the other partner kicks. Also, if possible, give each set of partners a different-colored ball. It is easier to remind them to retrieve a ball if you can refer to its color and is easier for them to track a ball of a particular color.

VARIATIONS

- Use fewer or more pins according to the group's ability level.
- Add more pins and keep a tally of pins down for each partnership.
- Increase the distance of the lines from the pins.
- Do not use partners for younger or lower-functioning groups; just have everyone kicking.
- Use this activity in a station or center for the general physical education classroom, with or without partners.

ADAPTATIONS

- Move the pins closer for the student who is blind, visually impaired, or in a wheelchair, and assist these students in retrieving the ball.
- Use a tethered ball for the student who is blind or in a wheelchair.
- Use mats or a wall behind the lines to keep the balls in the general area.
- Assist the student with SID. This may mean hand-over-hand instruction.
- Allow the students in a self-contained class to sit and strike the ball with their hands if kicking is too difficult for them at the time. Eventually you can advance the skill to kicking.

TEACHING NOTES

The students enjoy this activity and do not worry about keeping score, though some of the upper-level students will keep their version of the score. Most groups will participate in this activity for an unlimited amount of time.

EVERYBODY SCORE

PLAYERS

Large or small groups for all grade levels with modifications

AREA

Gym or outdoor area

SKILLS

Throwing, blocking, eye–hand coordination, cooperation

EQUIPMENT

Two large cones, lots of soft or Gator Skin balls, one or more boxes or hampers to hold balls, bowling pins

ACTIVITY

Set up a goalie area with two large cones on the baseline of the gym under the goal, and place the bowling pins between the cones serving as a goal. Place two or more hampers or boxes of balls on the free throw line of the basketball court. Choose one or two students to play the position of goalie. They will be guarding the pins. All other players will start next to the boxes of balls. On the "go" signal, the throwers take the balls from the boxes and start throwing the balls at the pins, and the goalies guard the pins. The teacher and paraeducators can stand behind the goalie area and roll the balls back to the throwers until all pins have been knocked down. Change goalies after all pins are down.

VARIATIONS

- Increase or decrease the distance between the throwers and the goal.
- Use fewer or more goalies.
- Have students kick the balls at the pins.
- Have students roll the balls at the pins.
- Set up more goals for the general physical education setting.

ADAPTATIONS

- Assist the student who is blind when he or she is throwing or playing goalie; this student will need lots of verbal communication. Use bell balls if available.
- Assist any student who does not understand the object of the game.

TEACHING NOTES

This game looks like chaos, but elementary and middle school students love it. Some students chose to play goalie throughout the game, which is easy to accommodate because the game requires multiple goalies.

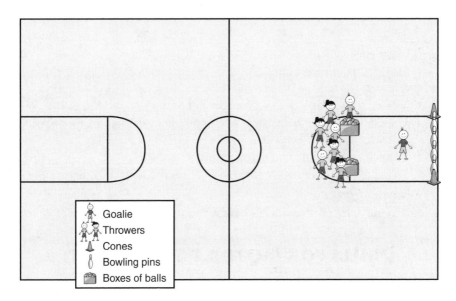

Goalie
Throwers
Cones
Bowling pins
Boxes of balls

▶ Everybody Score.

FIVE-HIT BASEBALL

PLAYERS
Small- or medium-sized groups for all grade levels with modifications

AREA
Gym or outdoor area

SKILLS
Eye–hand coordination, base running, throwing and catching

EQUIPMENT
Bases, plastic oversized bat and wiffle balls

ACTIVITY
Set up bases in the playing area and instruct students to take positions on the field. Choose a batter, who will be allowed to hit five practice hits before running the bases. Remind the batter when it is time to run. You will pitch the balls to the batter, and the fielders will retrieve the balls and return them to you. When the batter runs, the fielders will attempt to tag the runner.

Most students with ID do not comprehend the concept of base running and will need assistance, either verbal or physical. However, they love this game.

VARIATIONS
- Play the same game with a kickball.
- With smaller groups, give the batter 10 hits.
- Because of attention difficulties, with some groups it may be best to use only two or three hits with a more continuous rotation in batting and fielding.

ADAPTATIONS
- Roll the ball to the batter with poor eye–hand coordination to improve tracking skills.
- Use only one base for lower-functioning groups.
- Use hand-over-hand assistance for the batter with poor motor planning or for a batter who is blind.
- Push the wheelchair of a student with no mobility.
- Physically assist students with physical disabilities that hinder running.

TEACHING NOTES
I use this game for all levels of learners with varying degrees of adaptations.

DRILLS FOR MOTOR DEVELOPMENT

Using drills helps to teach skills systematically and allows the students to learn basic or specific skills before moving on to more advanced skills. Skills can be broken down into smaller increments, and one skill can build upon another to facilitate learning. Valuable motor development is enhanced through the use of drills to teach motor skills:

- **Gross motor skills.** Using the large muscles of the legs or arms is often difficult for students with disabilities to conceptualize, and they must be taught to exert energy in these muscle groups. For example, pushing and pulling are difficult tasks for them to perform and distinguish between.

- **Fine motor skills.** Gripping a bat or paddle, catching a beanbag, or pulling on a rope will improve weakness in the hand or finger muscles.

- **Locomotor skills.** Learning to hop, skip, jump, slide, gallop, or leap helps the student with motor planning and helps to develop fitness levels.

- **Manipulative or object control skills.** Learning to throw, catch, kick, strike, and dribble also helps with motor planning delays that the student may have, as well as increasing skill level for more advanced activities and increasing the student's self-confidence.

- **Memory.** Repetition of skills will help with memory struggles that the student may have. Repeating skills over and over during a drill will help the student perform the skill more naturally after a period of time. Understand that this time varies from student to student.

The following drills will help develop coordination, balance, body awareness, muscle tone, and motor planning skills. Most importantly, the drills will provide fun and encourage participation and effort rather than winning. These drills can be used for the main activity in the daily plan for students with developmental or cognitive delays, as well as in stations in a more inclusive environment.

For most of these drills, it is important to use verbal cues to aid with timing—for example, "1, 2, 3, catch!" Or use verbal cues to help students with motor planning to enable them to perform the task. The student with more delays may need hand-over-hand assistance to perform the skills. Nonetheless, fun will be had by all.

T-BALL PINBALL

Students will be hitting balls off large cones in an attempt to knock down pins. Use wiffle balls or small Gator Skin balls according to the students' level of readiness. Also, adjust the distance from the tee to the pins based on the students' readiness.

HOCKEY PINBALL

Setup is much the same as for T-ball pinball. The students attempt to knock pins down with a ball that they hit with a hockey stick or pillo polo stick. Adjust distance for students' readiness level.

FRISBEE TARGETS

Students use Frisbees to knock down pins or to hit inflatable targets. Frisbees may be too advanced for younger students in both general and developmental classes.

STRIKING SKILLS

- Students strike balloons or beach balls with their hands and progress to paddles (for lower-level students).
- Students use noodles to strike balloons or beach balls.
- Using bats and balls: Allow students to pitch the balls to other students who will practice batting. This works well in mainstream inclusion, inter-exceptionality, and general settings. Use hand over hand as a last resort when assisting.
- Using rackets and balls: Setup is the same as already described. This activity is great for eye–hand coordination. Start with paddles, progress to tennis rackets, and then to badminton rackets.
- With hockey sticks and polo sticks and balls: This is great for students who are unable to track thrown balls. The balls are rolled on the ground to the students to help them develop eye–hand coordination.

THROWING SKILLS

- Students are allowed to throw or roll balls at pins.
- Students throw balls or beanbags at targets such as boxes, inflatable targets, premade targets, large stacking buckets, or collapsible or folding targets.
- Students throw beanbags or balls with partners. Students with lower skills can use buckets or handheld fishing nets to catch the ball.

CATCHING SKILLS

- Start by having students catch beanbags and then have them progress to balls.
- Use large stacking buckets or small boxes for catching beanbags or wiffle balls.
- Have students use a small parachute or blanket to catch as a group.

KICKING SKILLS

- Students kick a stationary ball at pins as targets or use mini soccer goals as the target.
- Students kick a ball rolled by a partner.
- Students kick with a partner to work on kicking and trapping skills.
- Students chase a rolled ball and kick the ball. Use a target for students with readiness skills.

DRILLS FOR MID OR MOID STUDENTS IN MIDDLE AND HIGH SCHOOL

The following drills can easily be incorporated into the general physical education classroom and will benefit all students with or without exceptionalities. The drills can also be used as simple lead-up games for sports. They are very basic and develop skills such as chasing after loose balls or transitioning from offense to defense that may seem innate for general students as they start participating in team sports but must be taught to students with ID.

SOCCER DRILLS

ROLL, CHASE, KICK
Set up a soccer goal with cones or a mini goal, and line the students up approximately 15 or more yards (14 or more meters) from the goal. Roll the ball toward the goal and instruct the student in line to chase the ball and kick for a goal. The student then returns the ball to you, and you start the process for the next student in line.

Variations
- Add a goalkeeper.
- Increase the distance the ball will need to be chased.
- Alternatively, have another student kick the ball for the student in line to chase and kick.

Adaptation
- Assist students with physical, visual, or cognitive delays.

FIVE KICK
Set up a soccer goal with cones or a mini goal, and assign a student as the goalie. One student stands 10 or more feet (3 or more meters) from the goal and kicks five soccer balls (one at a time) at the goalie. The remaining students will be retrieving balls and setting the drill up for the next two participants.

Variations

- Increase the distance of the kick.
- Roll the ball to the kicker to kick at the goal.
- Set up pins for the goalie to protect.

Adaptation

- Assign two goalies to defend the goal.

BASKETBALL DRILLS

BONUS SHOT

Place three spot markers close to the basket, one on each side and one in the front. Allow the players to take turns shooting from the spots, and count each made shot as one point. The score is cumulative as a team score, not individual. Once a player has shot from each spot, the player is allowed a bonus shot (worth 2 points) from any spot on the court chosen by the shooter. The next player follows the same rules, and the player's score is added to the team score. This puts less pressure on the shooter and develops teamwork.

Variations

- Increase the distance of the shots.
- Increase the number of points scored for shots.
- Have the students take turns passing the ball to the players as they run to the spot before shooting.

Adaptations

- Lower the goal if needed and if possible.
- Use lighter or smaller balls for younger students or those having difficulty catching basketballs.

AROUND THE WORLD

Set up spots around the lane area from which players will shoot the ball. Play the game much like the original game; as a player shoots and scores, the player advances to the next spot. The goal is to score from each spot before the other players.

Variations

- Allow each player two attempts from each spot before moving on to the next player.
- Each player attempts a shot from each spot, and the group moves as a team and accumulates points as a team.
- Have players shoot layups instead of set shots and accumulate points as a team.

Adaptations

- Lower the goal if possible.
- Provide a lower goal or box for students to shoot at if they cannot reach the regular goal with their shots.

FOOTBALL DRILLS

DOWN, SET, RUN

Use two tall cones to set up a goal line approximately 30 to 40 feet (9 to 12 meters) in length. Instruct the students to line up about 50 feet (15 meters) from the goal line and provide each player a flag football flag or belt. Assign one student to play defense and stand in the middle of the playing area. The students in line will take turns running with the ball in an effort to score a touchdown. The teacher, peer, or paraeducator will be the quarterback who will hand the ball to the runner. The quarterback gives the prompts *down, set, hike* to alert the runner to start. Once the runner starts to run, the defender attempts to pull the runner's flag. The runner is allowed four attempts to score.

Variations
- The quarterback can pass the ball to the runner.
- Allow students to play the quarterback position.
- Assign more than one defender.
- Eventually add more than one offensive player.

Adaptation
Reduce or enlarge the size of the playing area based on the students' abilities.

DOWN AND OUT

Set up a goal area with two tall cones and instruct all students to line up in two even lines that begin approximately 30 to 40 feet (9 to 12 meters) from the goal. Place a spot marker halfway between the heads of the lines and the goal. On the "go" signal, have the first two students in line race to the spot, and throw a pass for the first student to the spot to receive. The other student will attempt to pull the receiver's flag as the receiver runs toward the goal to score.

Variations
- Add a defender in the goal area.
- Designate a student to receive the ball.

Adaptations
- Shorten or lengthen the playing area based on the students' abilities.
- Use softer, lighter balls that will be easier to catch.

ACTIVITIES FOR STUDENTS WITH SID/PID

Students with severe or profound intellectual disabilities will need more assistance than other groups with intellectual delays. Their social and motor skill delays will be much more pronounced than students who are MID or MOID, and they may have difficulty understanding the rules, objectives, or cause and effect of games. Their levels of intellectual and motor functioning are very basic. Many will have no communication skills, will have an extreme inability to stay focused, and most will be unable to perform motor skills without assistance. However, inclusive situations that provide parallel activities in a general setting or inter-exceptionality groupings have proven to be beneficial for some of my SID/PID students. My experience has shown that modeling and peer facilitation from higher functioning students is a positive and effective means of inclusion for students with SID/PID.

Skills within the curriculum can be broken down into simple tasks and the students' behaviors can be shaped as they complete the task. In a self-contained environment, when working on certain skills, I have found it helpful to work with each student individually while other students are using different equipment. Peers and paraeducators can perform this same technique or assist the other students. Some students are even able to interact within a group in a simplified game or activity, though they may not understand the rules or objectives of the activity. In addition, most students will respond to auditory, visual, and tactile stimulation.

- Use lots of verbal and physical prompts. For example, saying "1, 2, 3, throw" will help the student prepare to throw the ball.
- Use the hand-over-hand technique for assisting students with motor skills.
- Set up parallel activities on the sidelines, with peer facilitators to assist. Examples could be rolling the ball at pins or targets, throwing beanbags at targets, or performing stunts on mats.
- Use balloons and multi-colored beach balls instead of regular balls for throwing, catching, and striking skills.
- Use bell balls, multi-colored beach balls, or balloons for teaching tracking skills.
- Teach motor skill development by using the motor skill progressions from the rating scale for motor skills (table 4.1 on page 61).
- Provide activities that help the students acquire the independence necessary to sit, stand, and walk.
- Set up circle-type games and have the students roll balls at pins or throw beanbags at targets. The teacher, paraeducator, or peer facilitator can hold the target in front of each student attempting to throw.
- Allow the student with SID/PID to hold on to a tether or small ring held by a peer when attempting to run or walk fast during games and warm-ups if the student resists someone holding her hand.

- Set up mini obstacle courses for crawling, stepping over, stepping down, jumping, or climbing skills.
- Use large exercise balls for stabilization and for teaching students to bounce and engage their leg muscles.
- Plan multiple activities to compensate for their inability to stay focused.
- Tie ribbons or bells to striking implements to provide visual and auditory stimulation.
- Use musical instruments such as drums, shakers, and jingle bells for auditory and tactile stimulation, as well as motor development.
- Pull the students on scooters with a rope. If grasping the rope is difficult for the students, tether the rope to the handle of the scooter. This will help develop muscles in the back and abdomen.
- Use adapted equipment, switches, and computers to enable students to participate. The special education teacher, adapted physical educator, or technology specialist could be resources for incorporating these technologies.

CONCLUSION

Students with ID have varying degrees of intellect but can experience success in physical education and sport activities. This chapter has addressed the characteristics that may lead to these varying degrees of understanding and participation and has presented activities and tips to help physical educators include students with ID. Enjoy the loving nature of these students and experience their joy in being accepted by others. They truly want to be included and respected.

5

Including Students With Cerebral Palsy

Most of the students that you will encounter in general physical education with orthopedic impairments will be students with cerebral palsy (CP), significant developmental delays (SDD), traumatic brain injury (TBI), or students who have had a stroke. All of these students have damage to motor control areas of the brain (Porretta, 2005). Because the incidence of CP is higher, this chapter includes more information about this disability; but the modifications will often be the same for students with SDD, TBI, or stroke. In addition, the chapter on intellectual disabilities includes modifications for the student who has cognitive delays in conjunction with any of these conditions.

Cerebral palsy is a nonprogressive condition that does not worsen over time, but there is no cure. Depending on the amount of damage to the brain, symptoms vary widely, ranging from severe (total inability to control bodily movements) to very mild (only a slight speech impairment) (Porretta, 2005). Children with CP may have learning problems, verbal or receptive language struggles (or both), sensory problems with seeing or hearing, or intellectual delays or disabilities. Because the motor abilities of students with CP are compromised, they may also have problems with balance and fitness. If this is the case, the student will wear a protective helmet in case of falls. Students with CP can also have spatial awareness problems and struggles with being attentive (Porretta, 2005).

Some students with CP have spastic CP, which means they have tight muscle groups and their movements are stiff. These students scissor their legs as they walk and may have a hard time holding or letting go of objects. Others with CP have low muscle tone, which makes it difficult for them to walk or even sit up. This form of CP is called *athetoid CP* and affects the whole body, creating a mix of stiffness and involuntary movements. These students also have a difficult time holding or controlling objects. Another type of CP is called *ataxia*. Students with ataxia have a disturbed sense of balance and lack coordination for proper arm and leg movements, causing them to walk unsteadily (Porretta, 2005). Interestingly, some students may have a mix of these types of CP.

Because of variations in the degree of the condition, different parts of the body may be involved. Sometimes only the legs are affected by CP, and sometimes only one side of the body (arm and leg) is affected. However, both arms and both legs, as well as the torso, can be affected at the same time. Students with the least-involved body parts may limp slightly, while others may need a walker, crutches, or a wheelchair (Porretta, 2005). In addition, some students may have shunts and wear helmets to protect them should they fall or receive a blow to the head. Once again, it is important to communicate with the paraeducator or classroom teacher to determine any restrictions that the student may have.

As already noted, many students with CP have balance issues, and safety will be a concern. For the student who falls easily, I usually request that the parents provide knee pads or elbow pads for the student for physical education. I have even had students who wear knee pads all day under clothing; the knee pads are not noticeable. In addition, a gait belt can be used to support the student during faster-paced activities. The paraeducator or the teacher will need to hold on to the gait belt; no peers should be allowed to do this. The belt is usually an adjustable strap that Velcros or buckles around the student's waist and is no hindrance to the student at all.

I also allow other students to lend an elbow to the student with CP when running or playing different games. That is, the student with CP is allowed to hold on to another student's elbow, in much the same way as a student with a visual impairment would use a sighted guide. This allows the student with CP to maintain balance and alleviates the possibility of the peer attempting to catch the student with CP who is losing balance. In some situations the paraeducator may be the only person allowed to assist the student in this manner.

Other students with CP may use a walker because they have more severe impairments or balance and strength issues. I have found that

▶ Gait belt.

the walker actually increases the student's independence in many situations and allows the student to participate in more activities. Many students may also have braces or ankle-foot orthoses (AFOs) for support and stability, but often these are not an issue. I have had some students who could actually run with their AFOs on.

This chapter provides modifications for the student who is self-ambulatory to varying degrees and does not need a wheelchair for mobility. Chapter 3 presents the modifications for those students who need wheelchairs. However, in some cases the strategies overlap and the modifications are appropriate both for students in wheelchairs and for students who are ambulatory.

Many modifications can be used to enable the student with CP to participate in general physical education; however, in order to increase strength and fitness, to improve flexibility, or to develop range of motion, it is highly recommended that the general physical educator or adapted physical educator collaborate with the particular child's physical therapist. Effective teamwork for the child with CP needs to bring together professionals with diverse backgrounds and expertise. The team must combine the knowledge of all members to safely implement a plan for the child's services. Remember that the degree of the condition varies and that not all children with CP are the same. Therefore, certain exercises or stretches for the student with spastic CP would not be the same for the student with athetoid CP and could do more harm than good.

MODIFICATIONS FOR STUDENTS WITH CEREBRAL PALSY

The student with CP knows that he or she is physically delayed, and this can be very frustrating for the student. In my experience of including students with CP, though, I have observed that these students are willing to work very hard to participate. They seem to have an incredible desire to be a part of the general population. So, when modifying activities for the student, keep in mind that the student wants to participate, but that the expectations will be different from those for the general peers. I have found that if the modifications are remotely related to the general peers' activities, the student will feel included.

It is important to find the student's strengths and build on those strengths, as well as to work on improving weaknesses. For example, the student may have superior upper body strength and may enjoy pull-ups from a supine (on the back) position using a dowel held by other students, or the student may have good object control and may be able to play catch with a partner. In other cases, the student may have limited upper body strength and may need modifications for every activity, but enjoys interacting with others and can still participate with a peer with modifications.

In my opinion, it is of great importance to involve the student with CP in making decisions concerning how he or she would like to be included. Some students are more comfortable than others in inclusive situations; some are more aggressive when participating in certain activities. Many students are able to convey their comfort level in certain situations and will actually facilitate the inclusion process if given the opportunity.

ACTIVITY TIPS

The following tips are basic and easy to implement for the student with CP. If possible, allow peer facilitators to interact as much as possible with the student with CP during these activities. And, as mentioned in earlier chapters, it is important to ask the student before announcing any safety modifications or rule changes to the class as a whole. Most of these tips are also relevant for students who use walkers, but I have included extra modifications when needed.

Most importantly, allow varying degrees of participation and do not expect the student with CP to perform skills and activities perfectly. It is far more advantageous that the student perform activities as independently as possible. Promote the attitude that it is acceptable for performance to be at one's own ability level, and embrace all small successes.

Tag Games

- In tag games, allow the student with CP to accumulate tags (two or more) before being "out." You should inform the rest of the class of this modification by simply saying that the student gets three tags (unless the student with CP does not want the extra tags).
- If the student with CP is "it," allow him or her to use a fun noodle to tag others.
- Allow a peer to assist the student with CP in tagging others; especially if the student uses a walker, he or she needs both hands for support.
- Allow a peer to lend an elbow, if appropriate.

- In ball tag games, allow a peer to deflect balls for the student with CP. But **never allow balls to be thrown at a student with CP who has a shunt.** In this situation, balls can be softly rolled on the ground at the student. Also, balls should be rolled at the student's walker, aimed at the frame, and not at the student.

- Set up protective boundaries with cones to signify an area for the student with CP to stand in when "battle ball" types of games are being played. In addition, allow a peer or the paraeducator, or both, to deflect balls thrown at the student. Peers can rotate as the person who deflects balls so that they all receive sufficient game time. Again, allow only rolled balls toward a student who has a shunt; no balls of any kind should be thrown at the head.

Obstacle Courses

- Set up a parallel obstacle for the student with CP if an obstacle is too difficult.

- Allow a peer or the paraeducator to assist the student on the course, and allow the general peers to pass the student on a difficult obstacle with a kind warning.

- Allow a peer to lend an elbow, if appropriate.

- If the student who uses a walker also has a gait belt, which is likely, then the paraeducator can assist the student on the same obstacles that the general peers are using. For example, the student could transfer to do an under or over obstacle as the paraeducator holds the gait belt.

Relays

- Shorten the distance of the relay by moving the boundaries when it is the student's turn.

- Use tethered balls for tossing and kicking. Balls can be tethered to the student's body or the student's walker.

- Allow a peer to lend an elbow, if appropriate.

- Allow a peer to retrieve equipment when the activity is an object control relay.

- Push the student on a scooter during locomotor relays if the student has poor balance and has difficulty doing the relay. The student's poor balance could increase the chance of falls during these activities and the support from the scooter could lessen that chance.

- Assist the student when he or she is using ropes. The paraeducator or peer can control the rope for the student. Allow the student to step over the rope. Or, allow the student to twirl the rope on one side of his or her body.

Scooter Activities

- Allow the student extended time to participate, or give the student a head start. This may or may not need to be explained to the general peers.
- For relays or learning stations, allow the student to hold on to a rope or hoop that is being pulled by the paraeducator or a peer.
- Provide two attachable scooters to form a larger base for the student to sit or lie on. Sometimes the student's feet need to be propped on the scooter if he or she has lack of control in the legs.
- Always pull or push the student using a controlled speed, and convey this rule to the peers.

Catching

- Provide a prop such as a milk jug with the bottom cut out, a fishing net, a bucket, or a box for the student to use to catch small balls or beanbags.
- Give the student prompts such as *ready . . . set . . . catch.* This helps the student focus and prepare for the incoming toss. Because of motor delays, the student may have a 2- or 3-second delay in responding.
- Help the student prepare the hands or raise the arms for catching larger balls. Also, teach the student to trap the ball against the body if needed. A gait belt would be appropriate at this time for the student who uses a walker; the paraeducator could support the student in standing as the student practices throwing and catching. Or allow the student to sit if necessary. Some walkers actually have seats that pull down. With this type of walker, the back wheels automatically lock when the walker is pushed backward.
- Use a slightly deflated beach ball for the student to catch and trap.
- Use a tethered ball to enable the student to retrieve his or her own ball.
- Allow peers to assist in retrieving balls that are not caught or to catch balls for the student who has problems grasping.

Throwing

- Use prompts to help the student focus on the skill and to learn to sequence the steps in the skill of throwing.
- Use tethered balls to help the student retrieve unsuccessful throws.

- Shorten the distance of the throws.
- Use targets, pins, or buckets for practice in throwing skills. A peer may also join the student. (If throwing is too difficult, allow the student to roll the ball.)

▶ A tethered ball.

Striking

- Start with paddles and progress to rackets or bats.
- Use balloons for the student to strike to develop tracking skills.
- Provide hand-over-hand assistance for the student with poor upper body control for the student unable to track a thrown ball, or for the student having trouble grasping the paddle or racket.
- Use a progression of skills for striking: striking a stationary ball, striking a rolled ball, and striking a tossed ball.

- Students who use walkers may be able to strike with one hand off the walker because the walker locks if the student is leaning back on it. If the student does not have the strength to do this, then the paraeducator should assist the student.

Kicking

- Allow the student to kick a stationary or a tethered ball.
- Have the student kick with a partner who helps retrieve balls.
- For kickball, use a boundary that the ball must cross before the defensive team is allowed to field the ball, or have the defensive team count to 10 before fielding the ball. Then provide assistance for running the bases as needed.
- Develop a progression of skills for kicking: kick a stationary ball, kick a rolled ball, kick a bouncing ball, and kick a ball kicked by a partner.
- Tether a ball or empty milk jug to the student's walker to enable the student to kick with control.

Jumping Rope

- Start with a stationary rope for the student to step or jump over. Eventually, a peer or the paraeducator can swing the rope under the student as he or she steps or jumps.
- Have the student hold the end of the rope when others are jumping with long ropes. When it is time for the student with CP to jump with the long rope, have him or her step over the rope as others wiggle it.
- For jumping during a relay, allow the student to twirl the rope to his or her side while moving toward the finish line. Twirl the rope for the student who uses a walker.

Coordination Activities

- Modify jumping jacks by allowing the student with balance issues to perform jumping jacks using only the upper body. The student with a walker can perform jumping jacks using only the arms and using the walker for stability if the walker has a seat feature; if not, allow the student to do another movement such as lifting a foot several times.
- Modify toe touches by allowing the student to reach only for the knees if he or she is able. Some students may be able only to reach forward.
- Allow the student to sit when needed and to stand instead of sitting if he or she has difficulty standing from a sitting position.

- Assist the student with coordination problems during running by hooking your arm under the student's arm for support if no gait belt is available. Or, if the student has enough strength, have the student hold on to your arm much the same as if using a sighted guide for a student who is blind (see chapter 6).
- Students with walkers can run slowly if they are able; if not, walking is acceptable.

Fitness Testing

- Use the student's previous scores to compare from year to year versus using the fitness test scores of other students.
- Shorten the distance of the running events or allow the student to walk, and modify the time.
- Provide other means for pull-ups; for example, the student can use a dowel to pull up on while lying on a mat.
- Allow the student to grasp the hands of a peer when attempting sit-ups or crunches.
- Allow the student to perform the sit and reach with an object such as a pencil or ruler in the hands. This will ensure demonstrating a gain in flexibility, though the student may not be able to reach forward at all because of tight muscles resulting from the CP. Alternatively, allow the student to reach above his or her head if possible, and measure the distance from the shoulder to the reach position.
- Allow the student to step outward for the standing long jump, and record the distance.
- Allow the student to do wall push-ups or to use the bleachers and perform a leaning push-up.
- Allow a peer to assist the student in the shuttle run by picking up the object that the student is to retrieve.
- Allow the student to run using the wall of the gym for support if space is available. The student can touch the wall as he or she runs to compensate for balance issues. Also, I recommend that you shorten the distance in comparison to the general students. The student with CP may be able to run or jog just one lap around the gym for the mile run, but this is a great start.

Basketball

- Have the student practice dribbling from a sitting position, if needed, then practice while standing, and next practice while moving.

▶ Students prepare for the shuttle run.

- Have the paraeducator or peer facilitator help the student dribble by bouncing the ball in front of the student as he or she attempts to dribble.
- Have the student shoot at lower goals or handheld goals that can be manipulated to help the ball go through the net.
- Provide the opportunity for the student to participate in game play in one-on-one or two-on-two situations.
- Use drills to develop skills in small groups.
- If the student with CP has a shunt, avoid drills for rebounding to reduce the risk of the student's receiving a blow to the head. This may mean that the student will not be allowed to participate in game play but can practice dribbling, passing, or shooting at a temporary goal with soft balls with a partner on the sidelines.

Soccer

- Use a deflated ball for the student with CP to practice dribbling. This will slow the ball and allow the student to keep up.
- Use tethered balls if necessary or allow peers to retrieve the balls.

- Have students play games or perform drills in smaller groups.
- Allow a peer to assist the student with CP when he or she is playing the position of goalie.
- Give the student choices.
- Use drills to allow opportunities for the student to practice and develop skills.

Volleyball

- Have the student practice volleying with softer balls. Use balloons and beach balls for students with tracking skill problems.
- Toss the ball for the student attempting to serve.
- Use lower nets or no nets.
- Allow the student to catch the ball before attempting to return a volley. Or, allow a peer to catch the ball for the student with CP.
- Allow the student to throw the ball over the net.
- Have the student practice all skills with a partner or in a small group.
- Assist the student who uses a walker or provide a parallel activity on the sideline, such as volleying a balloon or beach ball with a partner.

Hockey

- Use a larger ball such as a wiffle ball or a beach ball for the puck.
- Use a tethered ball for the puck.
- Allow a peer to assist the student with CP when he or she is playing goalie.
- Have the student practice all skills with needed modifications with a partner or a small group.

PARALLEL ACTIVITIES

The following activities can be incorporated for the student with CP when the student is fragile and playing with general peers could be dangerous, or when the activities are not suitable for the student's ability level. Do not underestimate the importance of these activities for the student with CP. Because of their motor and coordination delays, repetition can be key in developing basic skills. For example, one of my middle school students learned to dribble a basketball by practicing this skill as a parallel activity. He literally started with one dribble and eventually was able to dribble one thousand times without stopping. This did not happen in a short amount of time, but he was happy to progress in small increments.

Elementary

- Have the student use paddles and balloons with a partner.
- Have the student throw at fun targets on the sidelines.
- Have the student throw and catch with a partner.
- Have the student practice kicking the ball with a partner or at a goal with a goalie.
- Have the student practice any sport skill with a partner.
- Tie a rope to a doorknob and allow the student to sit on a scooter and pull him- or herself with the rope.
- Have the student practice skills assigned by the physical therapist to improve flexibility, mobility, strength, or range of motion under the guidance of the paraeducator.

Middle and High School

- Have the student practice skills on the sidelines with a partner or small group.

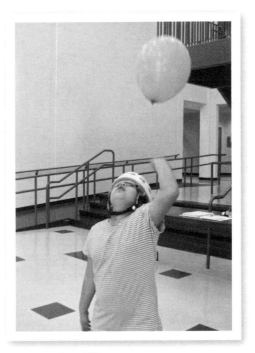

▶ Repetition is key to developing skills.

- Have him or her practice skills assigned by the physical therapist to improve flexibility, mobility, strength, or range of motion under the guidance of the paraeducator.
- Assign peer helpers who have been trained in the safety aspects of assisting the student.
- Give the student choices.

CONCLUSION

Providing an appropriate inclusive environment gives students with CP opportunities for enhancing social, emotional, and physical development. Of course, modifications should be made based on each individual's needs because of the varying degrees of impairment in students with CP, and it is important to remember to focus on the student's abilities. In addition, provide opportunities for the students to make choices and decisions in the inclusion process. Generally speaking, students with CP want to participate in physical education and enjoy interactions with their general peers, so be a part of the team and motivate these students to perform to their maximum potential.

INCLUDING STUDENTS WITH VISUAL AND HEARING IMPAIRMENTS

This chapter addresses both visual and hearing impairments. Students can be blind or deaf or have both impairments. In addition, some may have other disabilities along with either impairment. This chapter approaches visual and hearing impairments as the primary disability for provision of modifications. However, if the student has a secondary disability such as one requiring a wheelchair or even an intellectual disability, this too would need to be addressed and modifications would need to be adjusted accordingly. The first part of the chapter deals with visual impairments and includes helpful hints for facilitating the inclusion process; later sections discuss including students with hearing impairments.

INCLUDING STUDENTS WITH VISUAL IMPAIRMENTS

In general, *visual impairment* refers to any visual condition that interferes with a student's ability to perform everyday activities, and encompasses a variety of related terms. For the purpose of simplicity, I will use the term visual impairment (VI) to refer to a continuum of conditions including blindness and low vision. The student who is not totally blind but has VI that cannot be corrected is considered to have low vision. The term blindness generally refers to the lack of usable vision, and often the student who is blind is not able to see well enough to maneuver on his or her own (Spungin, 2002).

Each individual's abilities are truly unique because even people with the same VI can experience different degrees of vision loss. For example, some individuals may have reduced visual acuity, or a restricted visual field, or blind spots in their visual field, or high or low sensitivity to light; or they may have difficulty in distinguishing colors or contrasts. Some people may even have a combination of any of these conditions or a complete loss of sight. As you can see, students with VIs may vary widely in their ability levels because of the degrees of VIs (Spungin, 2002).

First and foremost, you want to feel comfortable teaching the student with VIs, and you want the student to feel comfortable in the environment of the gym. With this in mind, collaboration with the student's teacher or paraeducator can significantly improve the inclusion process and ease tension concerning the unknown. Under federal law, students who are visually impaired (VI) are required to receive special services from qualified personnel. For example, in my school system we have two main support personnel other than the classroom teacher and paraeducator of the student who is VI. Our teachers of students with VI, also known as vision specialists, oversee the student's Individual Educational Plan (IEP) goals and objectives and provide necessary modifications or special devices, and orientation and mobility (O&M) instructors teach students how to get around independently with the aid of special travel skills such as using canes and sighted guides.

I have found these professionals to be extremely helpful in introducing the student into the physical education environment and for providing basic guidelines for working with particular students based on their individual needs. Because of federal guidelines, I would assume that your school system employs professionals who are trained to do the same for your students. The best way to obtain this information would be to approach the classroom teacher of the student who is VI if you feel that you need assistance with the student.

The student who is blind or VI benefits not only in terms of physical fitness but also from the opportunity to socialize and have fun when included in physical education.

Again, it is advisable for the physical educator to talk with the teacher or paraeducator of the student who is VI about possible medical conditions that may restrict the student from certain activities. For example, a student with a detached retina should never receive a blow to the head. Therefore, it would be imperative that this student never have balls thrown at him or her or participate in a game such as volleyball, basketball, kickball, or baseball. In addition, this student should not run or jump, but should be allowed to stretch and participate in various activities in a safe environment that is monitored by the teacher or paraeducator.

Also, for the student who is VI, the paraeducator will be able to inform you about the student's *functional vision* or the distance that the student can actually see. Knowing the functional distance will aid you in providing modifications. In my experience, students with any functional vision at all attempt to participate without modifications. They prefer to blend in with the other students and do this very well. For example, I consulted with a student whose functional vision was only 6 inches (15 centimeters). The only trait that separated him obviously from his peers was albinism. Had I not known this, I would not have been able to determine that he was a student with VI.

It is equally important to talk with the student who is blind or VI to determine how much vision he or she has and to discuss any modifications that are needed. Some students with VI or blindness are able to see shadows, and some may even see colors. If the student has useful or partial vision, just using brighter or lighter balls may be the only modification needed. Or positioning the student so that he or she has a lighter background to face in order to track colored balls or other objects could be the only adaptation needed.

Overall, you will be in awe of the student's desire and ability to participate in physical education. The student who is considered VI with low vision will be able to participate in most of the same games and sports as sighted peers. The student who is blind will need more adaptations but will surprise you just as much in terms of the number of activities he or she can participate in when given a chance.

MODIFICATIONS FOR STUDENTS WITH VISUAL IMPAIRMENTS

The child who is VI depends on an increased amount of verbal communication. The student needs to be oriented to the surroundings and needs to know where he or she is with reference to these surroundings, as well as knowing the obstacles that may be present in the environment. The person communicating with the student should also convey his or her own movements to the student and **never leave the student unattended.** It is equally important that anyone approaching or leaving the area make this known to the student who is blind.

A peer or paraprofessional is needed to assist the student who is blind with mobility; this can be done in different ways with the peer or paraeducator as the "sighted guide." The student holds on to the guide's arm just above the elbow, with his or her thumb on the outside of the guide's arm and the fingers on the inside. The sighted guide should concentrate on staying one step in front of the student in order to set a cadence or rhythm. It is acceptable to allow younger, smaller students to hold on to the wrist or even the pinkie of the sighted guide (Spungin, 2002). Insist that the support person not pull the student through any activity. It is also important to realize that the lower-functioning or more cognitively delayed student will need more assistance, especially when attempting steps. Finally, it is important to train the sighted guide in use of the technique of guiding and to have the paraeducator monitor this interaction. Train the guide to give the student with VI very concrete and sequential directions. For example, the VI student needs to know where he or she is at all times and needs to know when to stop, turn, or step.

Another means for guiding the student who is blind or VI is to provide a tether for the student and the guide to hold. The tether should be a rope or strap with a loop on each end and should be no longer

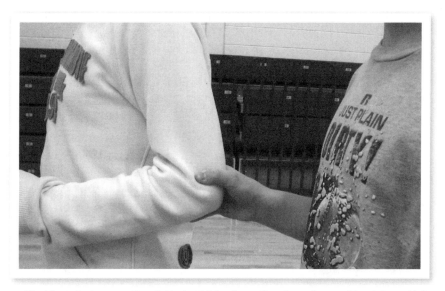

▶ The VI student grasps the sighted guide's elbow, thumb on the outside of the guide's arm and fingers on the inside.

than 2 or 3 feet (0.6 or 0.9 meters). The tether is helpful when the student is running in a controlled environment and has proper form. Again, monitor that the student is not being pulled through activities. Some students may never be comfortable with a tether, and others will love it. After introducing the tether, allow the student to choose either the sighted guide or the tethered rope for specific activities. Tethers work well for walking, running, and some locomotor relays.

Before allowing a peer facilitator to lead the VI student with a tether, it is important to train the student and paraeducator to use the tether. Basically, guides need to understand that they are not pulling the student rapidly through activities. The tether is provided to give the student some freedom and independence when participating in mobility activities such as walking or running. Speed is not the main objective but can be added if it can be attained safely. In addition, the guide should choose the safest path with the least resistance to lead the student through. During running, for example, the outside lane on the track or in the gym should be chosen to avoid having others cross the student's path, and obstacles should be avoided as the student moves around the gym or area. Communication is of the utmost importance in order to help the student feel safe and secure.

Use hand over hand (physical guidance), if needed, for the student who is blind or VI, but allow the student to do things as independently as possible.

Have the student choose whether he or she wants to participate with the group or do parallel activities on the sideline. Exercise is important, but the student's need to have a positive experience is an equal priority.

TEACHING BASIC MOTOR AND OBJECT CONTROL SKILLS

The younger child who is VI may need to be taught basic skills such as walking or running. The child who is blind can't model this from other students and may need instruction in spatial awareness and body concepts. Sometimes these students will run with stiff legs, possibly because of fear or a lack of opportunity. In this case it is important to stress to the child to bend and lift the knees while running. Again, the tethered rope works well for leading students during running because it gives the student freedom with the run.

Students who are blind or VI will need verbal cues when attempting to catch or throw a ball. For catching, teach them to prepare ahead of time with hands waiting and then to pull the ball to the body. Note that it is easier for them to catch a bounced ball because they can hear the sound of the bounce, and this provides a response time. (Use bell balls if they are available.) When throwing the ball, the student will need to be squared off to the direction of the target. The student should wear safety glasses when throwing beanbags or smaller balls with another student or with the class.

Use a stationary ball when you are asking students who are blind or VI to kick a ball, and realize that some of these same students may be able to strike or kick a rolled ball with bells. When balls are to be struck or batted, place them on cones or allow the student to strike a tethered ball. Tethered balls can be hung from a goal or any overhead support beam. In addition, larger tethered balls are now available that students can throw or kick at targets and retrieve themselves. Providing bowling pins to be knocked over with the balls also enables the student to receive feedback from the throw, strike, or kick.

Use ropes, cords covered with tape, or mats as boundaries or paths for getting from point A to point B for the student with VI. You may also clap your hands, blow a whistle, or beat a drum to guide the student to a particular point. Audible locators are also available that can be placed on goals or targets. Note, though, that these may be irritating to some students. Ask the student before using any of these auditory props which of them he or she would prefer.

ACTIVITY TIPS

The following tips will help your students with VI become successful in your physical education classes and will help you become more creative in developing further adaptations. Understanding your student's degree of VI will help you choose the ideas that will best meet his or her needs. In addition, this understanding will assist you in engaging peer facilitators in the inclusion process.

Tag Games

- For tag games with the student who is blind or VI, use a tethered rope (loop on each end) for guidance, and have the student run in the outside lane during group running or fleeing. It is also wise to teach the whole class to run in a counterclockwise path when playing tag games. Note that some students may not be comfortable with this because of spatial awareness issues and they will feel safer with a sighted guide.

- Allow the student with VI to use a fun noodle to tag others; this enables him or her to stay at a safe and comfortable distance and avoid contact.

- With ball tag games, instruct the other students that they must tag the student with the ball instead of throwing it at the student. This will reduce the possibility of tripping. (Inform the student with VI that you are communicating this adjustment to others.)

Obstacle Courses

- When using obstacle courses, have the paraeducator or peer facilitator guide or lead the student with a tethered rope.

- Use a sighted guide to provide assistance for the student on such equipment as the balance beam or in going over obstacles. If you hang ribbons or flags from the under obstacles, the VI student will receive sensory feedback and will know when he or she is actually under the obstacle.

- Use lots of verbal communication. Ask the student to stop, and then give the next direction, such as *step up, over,* or *under.*

- Provide individual obstacles for the student if necessary in a situation in which the student has a secondary disability that needs to be addressed such as cerebral palsy or spina bifida.

Relays

- For locomotor relays, use a tether for the student with VI or the student who is blind.

- Use a sighted guide.

- Allow two students to hold a long rope on the two ends, and have the student who is blind hold on to the rope to get from the start to the finish. Put tape on the end of the rope to signal that the finish is near, or use a cup or cylinder that will move freely down the rope for the student to hold on to during the run.

- For manipulative or object control relays, a peer facilitator or paraprofessional will need to assist the student in controlling the equipment. Again, verbal cues and signals will be necessary to orient and guide the student and help him or her manipulate the equipment. The peer will also need to retrieve loose equipment.
- Use a ball tethered to the student's wrist during tossing, catching, kicking, or dribbling and allow a peer to give verbal feedback.
- When equipment is involved, ask the student to participate in an outside lane so that there will be people only on one side.
- Peer facilitators can retrieve balls, beanbags, or other equipment when the student is waiting for a turn at the relay.

Scooter Activities

- Place the student in the outside lane during relays to reduce the chance of collisions. Many students who are blind, and especially those with VI, will be able to participate with the scooters and love to do so.
- Have the student sit on the scooter, and use a tether to pull the student if he or she cannot maneuver the scooter with the aid of verbal commands.
- Allow others to push the student on the scooter.
- Tie a long rope to a bleacher or a door at the end of the relay line or hold a long rope, and allow the student to pull him- or herself using hand over hand.

Soccer

- Use lead-up drills and games in order to include all learners.
- For soccer, a tethered lead will allow the student to run up and down the playing field.
- A peer will need to assist the student who is blind or has low vision in trapping the ball so that he or she may kick it while it is stationary. Verbal cues are important for indicating the direction of the kick.
- When practicing dribbling skills, the student who is blind or VI can hold the rope of a tethered soccer ball while kicking. The student who is blind will need verbal communication and mobility assistance.
- Tie an empty milk jug to a string for the student to kick in order to control issues such as travel distance or speed.

▶ A lower goal can help VI students in basketball.

- Deflate a soccer ball for kicking to reduce travel distance.
- Allow the student with more functional vision to assist another goalie.
- Use bell soccer balls.
- Provide small group drills if the student is unable to participate in the actual game.
- Give the student a specific task or duty in the game. For example, the peer or paraeducator can guide the student in running up and down the field, and once a goal is scored the student can be allowed to take a free kick at the goalie, alternating goalies each score. Or the student can be allowed to take a kick at a target to provide bonus points for alternating teams.

Basketball

- For basketball shooting skills, a lower goal may or may not be necessary for the student with VI; for the student who is blind, a lower or modified goal will be necessary.
- Audible locators or bells may help the student find the goal, but ask the student if he or she wants to use an audible device. Some students do not like the sound or the attention that it draws.
- Have the student practice passing and dribbling skills with a partner on the sidelines with the aid of verbal prompts.

- Use a lower goal.
- Use a makeshift goal such as a trash can or box to ensure success.
- For a basketball game, I recommend that a peer helper or para-educator assist the student in positioning, running, passing, shooting, and covering a defensive area.
- During a game, set up a drill on the sidelines or a mini game with peers who are waiting for the opportunity to play in the game. The peers can rotate in and out.
- Give the student a specific duty in the game after a scored basket. For example, the student could be allowed to take a free shot for a bonus for alternating teams or even attempt to hit a target or knock down pins for the bonus.
- Provide the opportunity for the student to run on the sidelines, or practice a skill, when awaiting the bonus duty.

Volleyball

- Use drills and lead-up games in order to include all learners.
- Lower the net for the student with VI if necessary during volleyball.
- Allow a peer to catch the ball and assist the student who is blind or VI in hitting it back over the net.
- Allow the student who is blind or VI to throw the ball back over the net.
- Use beach balls or brightly colored balloons, especially for the student with some functional vision.
- During game play, set up sideline or mini games with peers (who will rotate in and out) if the student who is blind or VI cannot participate in the game at a tolerable level or just chooses not to participate in the regular game.

Hockey

- Use lead-up or mini games in order to include all learners at all levels.
- For playing hockey, use a tethered lead for the student who is blind or has very low functional vision.
- Use a peer to stop the ball or puck; the peer will also verbally cue the student to hit the puck.
- For practicing dribbling, tether a wiffle ball to the hockey stick with a string (10-15 feet [3-4.6 meters]) so that the student doesn't have to retrieve balls; this allows some independence.
- A Frisbee with bells taped underneath can also be used as the puck.

- Use larger Gator Skin balls for the student to hit, and set up pins to be knocked down; the sound of the falling pins provides feedback that the student can't obtain visually.
- Allow students with some functional vision who are playing goalie to assist another goalie if needed.

Baseball or Kickball

- Have the student use a tee to hit the ball.
- Allow the student to kick a stationary ball.
- Set up an extra set of bases with a shorter distance, and use a tethered lead that will allow the student who is blind or VI to run the bases.
- Or, use a long rope stretched to first base for the student with VI to hold as he or she runs to the base. A simple way to do this is to have two people hold the rope for the student and drop it once the student reaches the base (the runner should be verbally cued that he or she is at the base, or tape should be placed on the rope to signify the end). The remaining base running will need to be done with a sighted guide.
- Have the student with VI use a tethered lead to run the remaining bases.
- Instruct the defense that they may attempt to get the student who is blind or VI "out" only after passing the ball to two other students.
- Make a boundary line that the ball has to cross over before the defense is allowed to field a ball hit or kicked by the student who is blind or VI.

Ping Pong

- Have the student with functional vision use paddles and balloons to play ping pong.
- For the student with no vision, use hand-over-hand assistance, or have the student hold the paddle in a stationary position as another hits the ball at the student's paddle. The student enjoys the sound and the vibration of the ball hitting the paddle and may soon attempt to push the ball back over the net once it makes contact with the paddle.

Cooperative Learning

- When teaching team building or cooperative learning activities, understand that the student with VI is accustomed to trusting others for his or her safety. Inform the other students to be prepared.

- Use blindfolds to help the general peers empathize with the student who is blind or VI.

- Allow the student who is blind or VI to be the team leader; the general students will start to recognize his or her strengths and to view the student as they do their general peers.

- Reinforce the importance of communication and of not leaving the student who is blind or VI alone.

Parallel Activities

The following activities can be used on the sidelines when it is not safe for the student who is blind or VI to participate in general physical education or if the student is not developmentally able to do so.

- Tie a rope to a door handle, bleachers, goal, or sturdy object and have the student pull him- or herself on a scooter to the end that is tied. The student may sit on the scooter or lie on two scooters.

- Have the student kick or throw a ball at bowling pins.

- Have him or her kick or throw a ball at brightly colored or contrasting-colored targets.

- The student can kick a ball at a goalie.

- The student can hit a beach ball over a lower net with a partner or small group.

- Put a teaspoon of uncooked rice in a beach ball to allow for auditory tracking.

- The student can throw at a large target. For example, set a gym mat on its side and allow the student with VI to practice pitching; the student will enjoy the sound of the ball or beanbag hitting the mat.

- The student can throw a Frisbee at pins while being given verbal cues from a peer or paraeducator (make sure that the peer is also taking a turn).

- The student can practice catching a ball thrown from a partner who is giving verbal cues.

- Have the student roll a ball with a partner, with both students sitting in V-position (recommended for elementary level or students with cognitive delays).

- Have the student hit a ball off a tee with a bat or racket (use pins to knock down; the student will like the sound).

- The student can hit a tethered ball with a racket.

- Have the student use a large tethered ball to knock down pins; the ball can be tethered to a goal or held in the nonthrowing hand.
- Have the student throw balls or beanbags at any targets that you may have (a box will work).
- Have the student practice sport skills such as shooting baskets, volleying, throwing or catching balls, kicking a soccer ball, or hitting a hockey puck with a peer or a group of peers on the sidelines.
- The student can play fun games with a one-on-one peer using bell balls. Line ball, for example, could be played with a partner. Set up two goals with cones approximately 3 feet (0.9 meters) apart, and have the students strike the ball with a hand in an attempt to make it cross over the opponent's goal line; the opponent tries to block the ball and in return attempts to score. The game is explained in chapter 8, "Walk in Their Shoes."

INCLUDING STUDENTS WITH HEARING IMPAIRMENTS

Students with hearing impairment (HI) have hearing loss that may fluctuate or may be permanent, whereas the deaf student is not able to hear at all and is not able to process linguistic information through hearing (Winnick, 2005). Both HI and deafness will affect students' educational performance, but students with these conditions can easily be included in an accepting physical education program. In addition, hearing loss or deafness does not affect the student's intellectual capacity or ability to learn. However, should the student have other exceptionalities, you will need to consider the primary and any secondary disability when including him or her. For example, if the student is intellectually disabled or is blind, obviously other modifications will also need to be addressed.

I will use the term *hearing impaired* (HI) to refer both to students who are hard of hearing and to deaf students unless the point relates specifically to either of these latter conditions. According to experts, members of the deaf community prefer the label *deaf* and are not sensitive to the term. They do not consider themselves "disabled" but rather members of a cultural and linguistic minority. Most do not want to be referred to in "person-first" terminology; a member of this community would rather be referred to as a "deaf person" than as "a person who is deaf" (Lieberman, 2007).

As with other exceptionalities, it is helpful to speak with the classroom teacher or the HI teacher in order to understand the degree of the student's hearing loss and to learn the best ways of communicating with the individual. In addition, attending the student's IEP meeting will provide the opportunity for you to meet and consult with the other specialist(s) working with the student. The IEP team can provide helpful hints for inclusion, means to communicate with the student, and instruction for using any communication or amplification devices that the student may need in the gym. Some students may even have an interpreter who is part of the IEP team and who would gladly assist the student in the gym if needed.

Some students with HI may have a cochlear implant and have unique needs that should be considered in physical education. For example, they should avoid sports that might result in serious blows to the head, such as football or basketball (rebounding), and should avoid activities that increase the risk of falls. However, with proper instruction and a secure means for storage, removal of the external part of the device will allow the student with a cochlear implant to participate in many activities, sometimes in combination with use of a helmet. But you should realize that removing the external part will result in complete hearing loss and the student may choose not to do this.

Hearing aids are also used by students with HI. Students may choose to remove their hearing aid in physical education because perspiration causes a "crackling" noise in the ear. If the student does want to remove the hearing aid, it should be stored safely and securely. On the other hand, should the student continue to wear the device, activities should be avoided that could result in blows to the head area.

MODIFICATIONS FOR STUDENTS WITH HEARING IMPAIRMENTS

For the most part, modifications for students with HI or deafness can be incorporated with little effort on the part of the general physical education teacher once the student has basic modifications in place or has reached a certain point in age and experience. Frequently, though, it is easy to forget to use these modifications because the student seems so typical in most ways. In any case, the following are some general hints for communicating and providing understanding for students with HI.

- Learn basic signs that the deaf student will need in the gym such as *stop, go, freeze, line up, wait,* or *yes* and *no*. When using a physical prompt to signal *go* or *stop,* I have found that the general peers are more attentive and respond well to the same signal.

▶ A visual scoreboard can be useful for students with hearing impairments.

- Use clear and consistent signals for starting and stopping activities.

- When students are playing games or doing other activities, use a scoreboard or a visual timer to keep score or to help the HI student keep track of the time remaining in the activity.

- Help the hearing students understand that if the deaf student does not follow the rules, it may be that he or she does not understand the rules—the student is not trying to cheat or gain an advantage.

- Keep a sign language book in your classroom to refer to when communicating with the deaf student. Such books will enable you to find a picture or sign for what you need the student to understand. I have also found it helpful to use the book when the student is signing to me and I don't understand.

- Use consistent signals to gain the deaf student's attention, such as touching the student on the shoulder or arm. Also, designate one peer who is allowed to do this for the student. That will decrease the possibility of several students approaching and possibly startling or overwhelming the student.

- Stand close to the student with HI or deafness and face the student when speaking so that he or she can see your lips. If the student does not read lips, this will at least signal your attempt to communicate.

- Demonstrate all skills so that the student can visually receive the information.
- Make sure that the student's placement in the gym allows the student with HI to see other peers and their performance of skills. For example, during warm-ups, it can be helpful for a student with HI to be a few rows back in order to model the skills that others are performing, although he or she does not have to wait for others to perform tasks and can actually be the leader or provide the modeling.
- Write down directions or information if needed. For example, providing a list of the class activities for the day will give the student an overall view or outline of the expectations for the class period.
- Write the list of the activities for the day on the dry erase board in the gym area.
- Assign a peer facilitator to assist the student. In some cases, this is the only modification that is needed. Train the peer to follow the suggestions listed here.
- For the student with residual hearing, minimize the background noise. For example, lower the volume when using background music.
- For the student with residual hearing, use bell balls to enhance his or her ability to track balls.

USING VISUAL AIDS

In my classrooms, visual aids have proven to have significant importance for deaf students. Because of their hearing loss, these students are essentially kinesthetic and visual learners. Therefore, I have come to realize the necessity for visual aids, especially for those who have any cognitive delays. Providing visual aids has given them understanding, and they have become active members of my classes.

Incorporating visual aids may prove to be somewhat involved, but remember that you can count on the assistance of other professionals who are knowledgeable about the student's educational needs. For example, some of the following visual aids may already be part of the student's daily plan and can be provided by his or her classroom or special education teacher. It is possible that you may need only to ask for assistance.

- **Visual timer.** Visual timers are clocks that do not tick and have no buzzers. When the timer is set on the desired time, the minutes are shaded in red and provide a visual countdown. Visual timers work well in activities performed in time increments or activities requiring time management such as stations, jogging, or games with time limits.

- **Visual stick.** Visual sticks can be designed based on the student's needs. The following photo shows a stick that I have used for my students, made from a large paint stick from the local hardware store and pictures that I acquired from the Internet or from the software programs Boardmaker or Writing with Symbols. I glued Velcro to the paint stick and to the back of the pictures so that the pictures can be alternated for different activities. The visual timer can be used in conjunction with the visual stick.

- **Visual stories.** Visual stories can be used in much the same way that Social Stories are used for students with autism. The visual symbols in the story provide pictures for better understanding

▶ This student removed each picture as he finished the task portrayed. This one modification increased his level of inclusion tremendously. He became less frustrated and started to participate with his general peers.

P.E.

1. Juan will exercise and run.

2. Juan will play basketball.

▶ A visual story.

for the student with limited skills. For example, the preceding visual story was used to inform a middle school deaf student with intellectual disability of the activities for the day in adapted physical education. Pictures replace the words that the student cannot comprehend. These pictures, along with the words, can help a student with reading and language comprehension and can be used just as well with students who have no cognitive delays.

The visual story was written using Boardmaker, which enables you to use single symbols as well as sentences as shown. I recommend that you check with the teacher of a student with HI; he or she may have a similar program and can assist you in writing visual stories. In this case, it would be necessary to provide the teacher with lesson plans ahead of time so that the visual story would be ready when the student arrived. Visual stories can also be stored in a folder or notebook for future use and can be used for your students with autism.

ACTIVITY TIPS

The following are tips for specific activities and are based on the general hints provided earlier in the chapter.

Tag Games

- Alert all students that no balls should be thrown at the HI student's head, especially if the student has a cochlear implant or a hearing aid; also provide a helmet, if possible, if this is acceptable to the student.
- Assign a peer to assist the student if needed.
- Use visual aids if needed, such as a visual stick, to demonstrate the game. For example, use pictures of the type of tag game (pictures of people tagging others or of balls being thrown as the tag).

Relays

- Demonstrate each relay and check for comprehension.
- Assign a peer to assist the student.
- Use a visual starting and stopping signal.
- Use visual aids such as listing the relays on the board, or use visual cue cards for each activity or relay.
- Initially, have the student with HI stand in line behind a peer as you demonstrate the relay, and eventually allow the student to become the line leader.

Obstacle Courses

- Demonstrate each obstacle.
- Assign a peer to assist the student.
- Post visual cue cards at each obstacle.
- Restrict or avoid obstacles that might cause the student with a cochlear implant to fall or perform weight-bearing activities on the neck or head area.
- Restrict these same obstacles for the student using a hearing aid, or assist the student in removing and storing the device.

Fitness Test

- Demonstrate skills.
- Assign a peer.
- Use scorecards to assist the student in recording scores for all events.
- Use a visual timer, scoreboard clock, or stopwatch to assist the student in timing the mile run, shuttle run, or flexed arm hang.
- Modify skill performance for students with cognitive delays in conjunction with HI.

Centers or Stations

- Assign a peer to assist the student in each station.
- Provide visual cue cards at each center or station.

- Provide bell balls if available for the student with residual hearing.
- Use visual cues for changing stations, as well as a visual timer.
- Provide a helmet for the student with a cochlear implant if available for stations where objects are thrown. If no helmet is available, have the student repeat a safer station instead.

Sports

- Restrict sports in which the student with a cochlear implant could receive a blow to the head such as football, basketball, hockey, tumbling, skating, soccer, and softball or baseball.
- When restricting these sports, plan lead-up games and drills for each sport that the student can participate in with modifications. For example, when performing a soccer drill, the student with a cochlear implant would never play goalie but could do controlled dribbling drills or kick soccer balls at a goalie in a controlled area. Or, for football drills, the student could throw at targets or throw balls to receivers who have been instructed to run the ball back to the starting point instead of throwing it back.
- Provide activity-specific helmets if available and agreeable to the student. However, if the student is not agreeable, restrict the activity completely.
- Use visual aids for the student with HI such as visual timers, scoreboards, or scorecards to manage time or scoring.
- Use colored jerseys to distinguish teams.

CONCLUSION

This chapter includes information both for students with VI and for those with HI. I suggest that you speak with the teachers of these students to determine the students' individual needs. Some students may need only a few modifications, and others may need many. Nonetheless, all are capable of participation and will benefit from the inclusion process based on their needs. Most importantly, be aware that other specialists are available to assist you in your endeavor to include students with visual and hearing impairments.

chapter 7

DIFFERENTIATION IN INCLUSIVE PHYSICAL EDUCATION

Differentiation is one of the most effective and successful methods of including students with disabilities in the general physical education setting because it focuses on building on each child's strength. More schools are starting to embrace the differences in all learners and understand the importance of planning for and implementing differentiation in classrooms. For schools that embrace inclusion, differentiation can be an effective method of ensuring a meaningful and successful experience for all students.

On a basic level, differentiated instruction is teaching with student variance in mind. Students enter our classes with different learning styles, skill levels, and interests. Therefore, planning for differentiation means starting with where the students are rather than adopting a standardized approach to teaching that seems to presume that all learners of a given age or grade level are essentially alike. Thus differentiated instruction is "responsive teaching" rather than "one-size-fits-all" teaching (Walsh, 2008).

According to experts, there are principles that guide differentiated classrooms, though there is no single formula for differentiation. In the differentiated classroom, multiple-option assignments are provided so that students choose the type of activity to complete, which supports the students' interests, learning styles, and performance levels (Tomlinson, 1999). A teacher can plan for differentiation by providing for one or all three of these. Some of the most obvious of these multiple-option assignments in physical education are learning stations, sequential drills for a skill or sport, and various lead-up games for differing abilities. Moreover, even in an activity such as relays, if we allow students to choose a particular relay or choose how to carry out the relay, we are differentiating. Many of us already teach this way; we need only to be more cognizant of our students' differences and provide varying levels for activities. When we provide these varying activities, our students soon recognize how they learn best and use this knowledge to expand on further learning.

Planning with differentiation in mind allows students to choose learning activities in order to support them in becoming self-reliant learners. Research shows that when learners are given choices, both the students' engagement in activities and their desire to participate increase (Tomlinson, 1999). This is definitely a priceless strategy for students with disabilities because it enables them to focus on their strengths. It also lends opportunities for other students to recognize abilities instead of disabilities as they see students with disabilities become successful during an activity.

Using differentiated instruction, physical educators can clearly include students with disabilities in general classes without hindering the quality of instruction for general students. According to experts, children seem to accept a world in which people are not all alike. In the differentiated classroom, these differences are considered for the basis of planning rather than viewed as problematic. The students learn to accept that not all students perform at the same skill level, and they are tolerant rather than critical. This can transfer to other life situations having to do with the acceptance of others' differences.

As physical educators, focusing on differentiation does not mean an entire shift from our present way of teaching; it means that we continue to strengthen our approach by teaching each child according to his or her individual learning style, skill level, and interests. We must place each student at the center of learning and plan lessons based on the different needs of students. By first meeting students where they are and assisting them in finding their own path to becoming successful learners, we build confident and independent learners (Walsh, 2008).

PLANNING FOR DIFFERENTIATION

Planning the differentiated classroom entails certain aspects that one would also consider when planning options for inclusion. Differentiation and inclusion go hand in hand, taking into account the strengths and weaknesses of the learners and compensating for all differences. One of the most positive perspectives of differentiation is that modifications and adaptations can be made for students with disabilities and that many of these same modifications or adaptations are appropriate for some general students.

The following discussion by no means covers all that the differentiated classroom entails. I have included some of the basic components that I consider necessary for any physical educator to use for differentiating the general physical education classroom. Many, many books include greater detail and provide more abundant information. I have touched only the tip of the iceberg and do not consider myself an authority in differentiation; however, I have found the following information essential based on material in *Teaching Physical Education in the Primary School* by Hopper, Grey, and Maude. Other work that I have found helpful is Walsh's article titled "Differentiation in Health and Physical Education."

When planning activities for the differentiated classroom, the instructor should consider the students' learning styles, which, according to researchers, can be classified as visual, auditory, or kinesthetic. Some students need to see the task performed; others can listen to directions; and many need to actually perform the task before they can learn or improve the skill. Moreover, the instructor must set up varying groups for the students to become a part of, provide diverse and mixed tasks with flexible outcomes, exercise the use of resources, provide authentic assessment, and manage student performance.

● **Grouping.** It is important to use flexible and varying groupings in order to meet all students' needs. The following groupings have been found to be successful in classrooms to address differentiated learning.

  a. Same-ability grouping can be used to develop or practice certain skills, as well as provide feelings of equity for all students.

  b. Mixed-ability grouping can be utilized to incorporate peer facilitation, which allows students to assume greater responsibility and take part in cooperative learning activities.

  c. Pairs grouping can enable students to work one-on-one with a partner for more personalized skill development and allows time for students to assess each other with greater confidence and accuracy.

  d. Individual grouping can also be utilized to provide opportunity for students to choose specific skills that they feel they need to develop and to provide time for repetition of these skills.

▶ Effective grouping can teach students a lot about teamwork.

Effective grouping of students can teach them to work as a team and to understand that all members can make varying contributions to the team. Again, students with disabilities feel included, and others see their abilities versus their disabilities. In addition, allowing friendship groups to form, through use of any of the groupings listed, can provide fun and enable students to relax and feel less intimidated.

● **Task and outcome.** Related but different tasks can be presented to account for differing abilities of the learners, providing activities for all levels. For example, an instructor could set up the following stations for kicking a soccer ball:

- Kicking a stationary ball at a target
- Kicking a ball rolled from a partner back to the partner
- Kicking a ball at a target with a goalie
- Kicking a stationary ball against the wall in the gym

Providing open-ended tasks can allow the students to interpret and achieve the task at many different levels for different outcomes. For example, an instructor teaching a cooperative learning activity would provide varying equipment for a group to move the whole team from point A to point B. Different levels of challenges can be presented, and each group could possibly meet the challenge in a completely different way.

● **Resources.** Prepare ahead of time for the necessary accompaniments for instruction. Provide a variety of equipment for different abilities. For example, to teach striking skills in stations, use balloons for students with lower tracking skills, shorter rackets for students with somewhat higher tracking skills, and longer rackets with a ball for students with even higher tracking skills. Provide a variety of equipment or apparatus for levels of experience as well. For example, if you are teaching tumbling, provide a wedge mat for students new to tumbling; for the experienced tumbler, provide only a mat for rolls, or add a balance beam or vault for the experienced gymnast.

● **Assessment.** My recommendation for assessing students in the differentiated classroom would be to incorporate some type of authentic assessment in which all learners are evaluated in game-like and applied settings rather than in artificial test situations. For example, rubrics can be developed that include levels of affective and cognitive attributes as well as task analysis. These rubrics can be used during games, centers, lead-up games, or actual sport participation. All learners can be assessed on skill development, knowledge, problem solving, and rules of the game. You can simply add more levels to the upper or lower end of the rubric to accommodate for differing abilities. Most importantly, these assessments give feedback during instructional time and during teaching units, so adjustments can be made by both the teacher and the students.

• **Managing student performance.** Though the students in the differentiated classroom are often allowed to choose their activities, the teacher must remember to provide for performance levels, interests of learners, and their learning styles. The teacher still observes the learners and provides feedback or reteaches skills, and encourages students to observe each other's work. With respect to learning styles, the teacher provides directions and verbal cues for the auditory learners, demonstrates skills or diagrams skills on the white board for visual learners, and provides walk-through or practice for the kinesthetic learners.

Throughout the lesson, the teacher scans for task compliance; the students are developing the skill of self-discipline in the area, and it is imperative that the teacher monitor for this. The teacher also handles discipline for the classroom; though the students will naturally learn to problem solve, the teacher cannot expect them to resolve all disagreements or conflicts. Additionally, when allowing the students to take on these roles and responsibilities, the teacher must consider safety in planning class activities. Students will be performing at differing ability levels and may need assistance in choosing proper equipment or activities. Also relative to safety, the teacher must monitor that all students are following the guidelines and resisting the temptation to clown around or roughhouse.

ACTIVITIES FOR THE DIFFERENTIATED CLASSROOM

The following activities are sample lesson plans for a differentiated classroom that will enable students with disabilities, as well as students with lower skill levels, to participate. Sample plans are provided for all grade levels—elementary, middle, and high school. Many of the activities are interchangeable and can be adapted for other grade levels. These are only samples to provide ideas for your classroom, and represent just a few of the many fun activities that you can plan for your students of varying abilities. Understand that the activities can be differentiated even more for higher-level students who require more rigorous activities. And note that with station activities, a management system for changing stations needs to be in place to maintain order in the class.

Adaptations are included that will enable students with disabilities to participate more effectively. However, because of the differentiated activities, most students—whether they are able-bodied, developmentally delayed, orthopedically impaired, or blind or whether they have autism—will be able to participate. Additionally, variations are suggested for differentiating instruction.

OBJECT CONTROL STATIONS (ELEMENTARY)

In object control stations, the simplest means of changing is for the students to stay in each station for a certain amount of time and rotate to a new station on the signal given by the teacher. Once the students rotate, they have different choices in each station. The differentiated choices include various types of equipment, skills, and groupings. Within each station, the students are allowed to practice one or all of the choices based on availability and time.

STATION 1: THROWING SKILLS
Students choose one of the options in the station and understand that it is permissible to rotate to the other options:

- Throwing objects of choice (football, playground ball, or Frisbee) with a partner
- Throwing balls or beanbags at a target
- Throwing a Frisbee at bowling pins set on a table, bleacher, or box

STATION 2: STRIKING SKILLS
Students choose one of the options in the station and understand that it is permissible to rotate to the other options:

- Striking with a plastic bat at a foam ball thrown by a partner
- Striking a tethered ball hung from a rope line or from the goal with a bat or racket
- Striking balloons with the hand or a racket with self, partner, or a group in circle formation
- Striking a small ball off a cone with a bat or racket in an attempt to knock down pins or empty tennis ball cans

STATION 3: KICKING SKILLS
Students choose one of the options in the station and understand that it is permissible to rotate to the other options:

- Kicking a soccer ball, balloon, or playground ball with a partner
- Kicking a soccer ball, balloon, or playground ball in a group circle (a defender in the center of the circle can be added by choice)
- Kicking a ball at bowling pins or other targets
- Kicking a tethered ball to practice control skills with self or a partner

STATION 4: ROPES

Students choose one of the options in the station and understand that it is permissible to rotate to other options:

- Jumping with a short rope
- Jumping with a long rope with a group
- Jumping using a jump stick with a partner; the partner twirls the stick with the rope for the jumper to jump
- Jumping while running in a specified area
- Practicing partner or group stunts with short or long ropes

ADAPTATIONS

- Adjust throwing distances.
- Provide an object to aid the student with catching skills, such as a box, bucket, or net.
- Use tethered balls for catching, striking, and kicking skills if needed.
- Use spot markers to help students with autism stay on task.
- Use bell balls, if available, for the student who is blind.
- Allow peer facilitators to assist students with disabilities.

VARIATIONS

- Set up stations with fewer options.
- Set up stations on consecutive days and rotate by day instead of at intervals within each class time.
- Use one station for the whole class on any given day.

ASSESSMENTS

Provide a checklist or rubrics for partners to use to check off skills that each partner has practiced or mastered, or allow individual self-assessment.

FITNESS STATIONS (ELEMENTARY AND MIDDLE SCHOOL)

In the fitness stations, the teacher manages the process of changing stations according to the time alloted for the class and the number of students in each class. For example, for groups with fewer students, the teacher may choose to have the students participate in all stations during a single class period. Or, for larger groups, the teacher may instruct the students to participate in only one station as a warm-up before the planned daily activity and to rotate to a new station the next day.

The students will decide to participate within each station alone, with a partner, or in a group with a leader. Partners or leaders will be responsible for using timers and for leading the groups through each station. For example, a student leader may lead the stretching exercises or the crunches.

STATION 1: OBSTACLES

Set up a short obstacle course (four obstacles that the students must crawl under or jump over). Have a row with lower obstacles and one with higher obstacles. The students have a choice of either course and a choice of whether to race another student on the other obstacle. Or, students are allowed to use a stopwatch to time themselves or others.

STATION 2: SCOOTERS

Students may choose any option in the station and understand that it is permissible to rotate to another option if time permits or the option is available:

- Traveling in a zigzag motion on the scooter through cones in a vertical line
- Pushing another student on the scooter in a specified area
- Pulling oneself on the scooter with a rope tied to a door or a bleacher
- Practicing scooter relays in a specified area; examples of relays are lying on one's stomach on the scooter and using the arms to maneuver, kneeling on the scooter and using one's arms to maneuver, or sitting on the scooter and using the legs to maneuver backward

STATION 3: JOGGING

Students may choose any option and understand that it is permissible to rotate:

- Jogging in place with a timer alternating slow, medium, and fast
- Jogging around a specified area for distance, time, or both
- Practicing the shuttle run from the President's Physical Fitness Test with the group or a partner

STATION 4: STRENGTH TRAINING

Students may choose any of the options, first understanding that they are allowed to rotate to each option if space is available.

- Crunches
- Push-ups
- Pull-ups
- Stretching, using a chart of stretches for the total body
- Use of light weights or stretch bands

ADAPTATIONS

- Adjust distances for jogging, scooters, or shuttle run.
- Allow students in wheelchairs to do wheelchair push-ups (page 47) and touch toes for crunches.
- Use spot markers to help students with autism to stay on task.
- Use a sighted guide or tether for the student who is blind.
- Monitor any student using the light weights.
- Add or delete obstacles for varying groups.
- Allow peer facilitators to assist any student with a disability or delay.

▶ Partners do push-ups.

VARIATIONS

- Substitute more or less difficult fitness options in the stations.
- Adjust the time in each station to fit the needs of the class.
- Assign students to particular options of the station based on the students' strengths and needs.

ASSESSMENT

Checklists or rubrics with varying levels can be provided for the students to record levels of mastery for each skill and fitness level.

HOCKEY SKILL STATIONS
(ELEMENTARY AND MIDDLE SCHOOL)

STATION 1: PASSING

Students choose an option for the station based on strengths or needs and understand that it is permissible to rotate:

- Each student has a hockey stick and shares a ball or puck with a partner for passing back and forth.
- Passing through cones: Partners pass back and forth using the cones as a pass-through target or gate for a more controlled passing drill.
- A small group forms a circle: One student stands in the middle and passes to each player; then players alternate being in the middle.
- Students pass to a partner while dribbling in a designated area.

STATION 2: DRIBBLING

Students choose an option for the station based on strengths or needs and understand that it is permissible to rotate:

- Dribbling through cones in a vertical line
- Dribbling in a designated area and passing to a partner
- Dribbling and shooting at the goal, attempting to hit a mat or the wall behind the goal
- Dribbling and shooting at the goal with a goalie in the goal to block shots

STATION 3: SHOOTING

Students choose an option for the station based on strengths or needs and understand that it is permissible to rotate:

- Dribbling and shooting at the goal; add bowling pins for the shooter to knock down
- Dribbling and shooting at the goal with a defender
- Dribbling and shooting at the goal with a defender in the playing area who is attempting to block or intercept the pass, as well as a goalie protecting the goal

ADAPTATIONS

- Use shorter hockey sticks for students in wheelchairs.
- Push students in wheelchairs.
- Make sure that a student who is blind uses the station with the pins to obtain feedback on the shot taken at the goal.
- If needed, set up an extra goal within the station for the student who is blind.
- Use spot markers for the student with autism who has a difficult time staying on task.
- Use tethered balls for the student who is orthopedically impaired or the student in a wheelchair to help with ball control skills.
- Allow peer facilitators to provide assistance to any student who needs it.

VARIATIONS

- Assign students to stations based on abilities.
- Use more or fewer stations based on space and need (outside playing fields provide more room for station setups).
- Set up a rotation schedule for the stations and signal the change for the stations.
- Allow students to monitor the time change and signal.

ASSESSMENT

Provide a rubric or checklist for partner or self-assessment of skill levels, knowledge, rules, and behavior.

SIDELINE HOCKEY
(ELEMENTARY AND MIDDLE SCHOOL)

Select a playing area and a playing field. Divide the students into two teams. The students will be stationed on the sidelines with their team members. In addition, assign each student a number. When their numbers are called, students enter the playing area to play one-on-one or two-on-two. The students on the sidelines keep the puck in play while the players on the inside are playing the game. Add goalies to the goals based on student readiness. Switch players every 2 to 3 minutes based on students' fitness levels.

ADAPTATIONS

- Push the student in a wheelchair.
- Allow a peer student to participate in the drill using a scooter when playing against the student in a wheelchair.
- Give verbal prompts to students with autism and allow a peer to facilitate.
- Use a tethered ball for the student who is blind; take away the other player serving as a defensive player, and allow the student who is blind a certain amount of time to attempt to score. Put bowling pins across the goal to give the student feedback on the score, or have the sighted students announce the score loudly.

VARIATIONS

- Adjust playing time based on readiness or fitness levels.
- Adjust the number of players based on readiness levels of the players to incorporate more defensive players.

ASSESSMENT

Provide drill-specific rubrics or checklists for partner or self-assessment for skill mastery or for rule and game understanding.

BOX HOCKEY
(ELEMENTARY AND MIDDLE SCHOOL)

Set up a playing area consisting of four boundaries that form a box. The boxed area should be approximately 30 feet (9 meters) square. Divide the students into four teams, with each team stationed on a different boundary line, and assign each student on each line a number (e.g., 1 through 10) based on the number of players. Place four pucks or balls (based on student readiness) and four hockey sticks in a center circle approximately 4 or 5 feet (1 or 1.5 meters) in diameter. In the middle of the circle place a bowling pin. When the student's number is called, the student will race into the center, grab a stick, and race around the outside of the square in a counterclockwise direction dribbling the puck. Once the student returns to his or her spot on the boundary line, he or she attempts to knock down the pin in the middle with the puck in order to

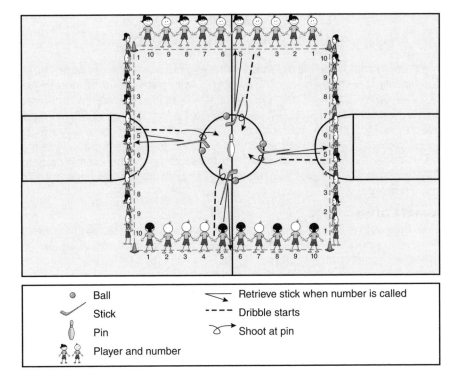

○ Ball	↘ Retrieve stick when number is called
⌣ Stick	---- Dribble starts
🎳 Pin	↗ Shoot at pin
🧍🧍 Player and number	

▶ Box Hockey.

score a point for the team. After a turn at play, each student resets the circle area, and a new number is called for the next player.

ADAPTATIONS
- Use a tethered ball for the student who is blind or orthopedically impaired and has trouble with controlling the dribble; the tethered ball can be attached to the stick or held by a peer.
- Push the student in a wheelchair who needs assistance.
- Provide verbal prompts for the student with autism.

VARIATIONS
- Set up different games for varying levels of student performance.
- Increase or decrease the size of the box based on the number of players or on skill levels.

ASSESSMENT
Provide drill-specific rubrics or checklists for levels of skill mastery performed by partner or self, as well as assessment for knowledge of rules and game strategies.

LAYUPS
(MIDDLE AND HIGH SCHOOL)

The participants divide into two lines, one on each side of the basketball goal. The activity is performed as a group activity, with each group scoring points for every shot made by a member of the group. Play starts with the students on the right side shooting and those on the left side rebounding. As students perform the skill, they switch sides of the lane. Each team continuously shoots and rebounds for a specified amount of time (3-5 minutes). At the end of the time allotment, the students record the team score so that they may compare the team scores after each time allotment. The goal is to see an improvement in team scores.

ADAPTATIONS
- Provide a lower goal for the student in a wheelchair or for the student who is orthopedically impaired, or allow a score for a ball that touches the rim or backboard.
- Assist the student who is blind with mobility and provide verbal prompts for shooting, also using the rule that the student scores if the ball touches the rim or the backboard.
- Use spot markers for students with autism who are having difficulty staying on task.

VARIATIONS
- Increase or decrease the time allotment based on student readiness.
- Have the students attempt set shots versus layups.

ASSESSMENT
Provide scorecards for team scoring and a checklist or rubric for individual skill assessment.

3 ON 2
(MIDDLE AND HIGH SCHOOL)

Instruct the students to form two groups; one is the offense and will have three players, and the other is the defense with two players. The offense starts about 20 feet (6 meters) or more from the top of the key, with one player in the middle as the point guard and players on the two sides as the offensive guards. The two defensive players set up in the lane area, with one player covering high (around the free throw line) and the other covering low (under the goal). The object is for the offense to attempt to score and the defense to keep the offense from scoring. The three-on-two setup allows the possibility for one player to be open (unguarded) and hopefully attempt a shot. The defending players learn to move around and defend more than one player, somewhat as in playing a zone defense. If the offense scores, the defense stays on defense and three new offensive players approach. Should the defense obtain the rebound from a missed shot, the shooter is eliminated and the defense becomes the

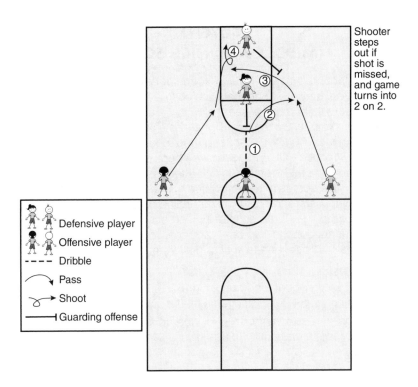

Shooter steps out if shot is missed, and game turns into 2 on 2.

Defensive player
Offensive player
- - - - Dribble
Pass
Shoot
Guarding offense

▶ 3 on 2.

offense versus the two remaining original offensive players, who then become defensive players, in a two-on-two situation. Play is over once someone scores; the original two offensive players now become the defense, and the original defensive players rotate to the offensive lines. This can be confusing, and a teacher, paraeducator, or student may need to monitor and assist students in changing positions.

ADAPTATIONS
- Assist any players who do not understand the drill.
- Set up a one-on-one drill for students who are unable to participate.

VARIATIONS
- Instruct the defensive players to stay on defense until asked to rotate; there is no two-on-two situation.
- Limit the number of shots that can be taken to determine when play is over. For example, after three missed shots, play is over and players rotate.

ASSESSMENT
Rubrics can be provided that depict skills, knowledge, and behavior.

GOTCHA
(MIDDLE AND HIGH SCHOOL)

Instruct the students that all players except for one will be eliminated by the end of the game; they are to concentrate on free throws and layups. All players form a vertical line on the free throw line; the first two players will start, each with a basketball. On the "go" signal, the first player shoots a free throw; if this player makes the shot, he or she rebounds, throws the ball to the next player in line without a ball, and goes to the back of the line. If the first shooter misses the shot, he or she rebounds and attempts to make a layup before the next person in line scores a free throw or a follow-up layup. If the first shooter scores the layup before the next person in line scores, then he or she goes to the back of the line. If the shooter behind scores the free throw or layup first, he or she announces "Gotcha," and the original shooter is eliminated. Play continues in this sequence until all players but the finalist are eliminated.

ADAPTATIONS
- Provide a lower goal for students in wheelchairs or students with other disabilities, or set up a mini game on the sideline with few players.
- Allow the paraeducator or a peer to rebound for students who do not understand the game and to assist a student in shooting if needed.

VARIATIONS
- Assign fewer students to each game.
- Use a timer and shorten the game time to ensure more winners; this also may possibly force players to increase their speed, which will improve cardiovascular endurance.

ASSESSMENT
Allow students to assess skills and knowledge using a rubric or checklist.

CONCLUSION

As you can see, the differentiated classroom is conducive to the student's individual needs, which is also the best way to design inclusive instruction. Most of us use differentiated instruction on a daily basis and may not need to make any changes in our normal routine in order to achieve differentiation. However, if you need to add a few modifications in order to provide differentiated instruction, know that your students will respond well to these changes and will become self-confident in accepting the responsibility of making choices that involve how they learn best.

WALK IN THEIR SHOES: GAMES FOR UNDERSTANDING

Students without disabilities need to learn to understand and accept students with disabilities as well as other members of the classroom. This acceptance does not occur simply because students with disabilities are in these classrooms, but must be nurtured by an open and supportive teacher. I believe that the first step in this process for physical educators is to believe and accept that students with disabilities have a right to be included in the general classroom. Next, physical educators must assist the general students in empathizing with others who are different. Finally, inclusion provides opportunities for discussing differences in all students that may not otherwise be provided.

The activities in this chapter provide opportunities for this empathy to surface. Not only will the general peers have fun; they will also start to understand some of the challenges that students with disabilities face in their everyday lives. This became apparent to me while teaching an inclusion class that consisted of adult learners. Though they were accustomed to being the support persons for their students with disabilities, until the class they had never put themselves in their students' shoes. They gained a real understanding of what their students go through in everyday activities, and it was obvious that change had occurred. They became more tolerant and caring, and they understood their personal roles better in relation to support. The improved attitudes and levels of compassion were evident, and a permanent, significant shift had occurred.

As you include students with disabilities in your classes and guide the process of inclusion, general peers become more and more caring, giving, and tolerant of others' differences. They learn to recognize abilities instead of seeing the inability in others and therefore become more responsible citizens. Put-downs and criticisms cease to exist in these classrooms, and all students have respect for themselves and others. The classroom environment becomes a safe and inviting place for all learners.

ACTIVITIES

The following activities are designed to develop empathy.

SORE SPOT TAG

LEARNING EXPERIENCE
Understanding physical impairments

EQUIPMENT AND MATERIALS
None

DESCRIPTION

This is a tag game in which everybody is "it." On the "go" signal, all players start walking and attempt to tag others. Once a player is tagged, that player has to touch and hold on to the spot on the body where he or she was tagged, and this becomes a "sore spot." Once a player is holding a sore spot, he or she cannot move the body part that is holding it. For example, a player who is tagged on the back reaches back and holds the tagged spot with a hand and is not allowed to use that hand to tag others. Most players are able to hold two or three sore spots, which allows them to continue to play several times without being eliminated. A player who has no more options for holding a sore spot is "out."

SAFETY ISSUES

- If you allow players to use their feet to tag others, remind them not to kick in order to tag and that there is no tagging with the feet above the knee.
- No running.
- After a player is eliminated, he or she must step out of the playing area if the group is large.

VARIATIONS

- Allow students to stop in one location and tag others once they have been eliminated.
- Play the same game without the sore spot; instead have the players put one of their hands in a pocket and play with only one hand.

▶ Sore Spot Tag.

DISCUSSION QUESTIONS
- How did your sore spots limit your ability to play?
- How was your ability to maneuver affected?
- Did you feel equal to others?

CYCLOPS TAG

LEARNING EXPERIENCE
Understanding visual impairments (VI), peripheral vision impairments, and hearing impairments (HI)

EQUIPMENT
None

DESCRIPTION
Instruct students to choose a partner and decide which partner will start as "it." Next, explain that each player is a cyclops, which means that each player will close one eye and form a circle with the hand around the other eye. The cyclops is blind in one eye, and the other eye has no peripheral vision. Have the partners spread out around the gym, and on the "go" signal, the "it" player will attempt to tag his or her partner. There is no running, only fast walking. Once tagged, a player becomes "it" and attempts to tag his or her partner. The game goes back and forth with partners alternating being "it," and continues until you call "stop."

SAFETY ISSUES
- Remind students that there is no running.
- They should use their extra hand as a bumper to avoid bumping into another person.
- "It" should gently tag partner; no pushing.

VARIATIONS
- Divide the class and play several 3- to 5-minute games versus one longer game.
- Provide headphones for a few students to simulate a hearing impairment.

DISCUSSION QUESTIONS
- Was this difficult for you?
- How does it feel to be VI?
- What strategies, if any, did you use?
- How important was your ability to hear?
- Were you hesitant or afraid?

LINE BALL

LEARNING EXPERIENCE
Understanding VI

EQUIPMENT AND MATERIALS

Bandannas for blindfolds, goggles partially covered for VI, bell balls or Gator Skin (soft) balls, cones for boundaries

DESCRIPTION

Instruct the players to form two teams; teams sit facing each other in two horizontal lines that are approximately 30 feet (9 meters) apart. Players in the lines should be about elbow distance from one another. Have each player wear a blindfold or goggles. The object of the game is to strike a ball with one's hand in an effort to get it to cross over the opponent's boundary line. Each team starts with three or more balls. Sighted players stand behind each line and retrieve or keep balls in play. Do not allow players to throw the balls; only striking is allowed. Bell balls work best, but Gator Skin balls will also work.

SAFETY ISSUES

- No throwing balls, as players could easily be hit in the face.
- Retrievers are needed for safety to communicate and oversee the game.
- If the class is large, break the group down and have smaller groups play several games at once.

VARIATIONS

- Allow a few players on the line to maintain sight.
- Adjust the distance between lines according to players' abilities.
- The game can be a sideline game played by two to four players with smaller boundaries.

▶ Line Ball.

- Provide earplugs or headphones for a few students to simulate HI instead of having all students VI.
- Allow the students to roll the ball instead of striking it. This can be an issue for younger students.

DISCUSSION QUESTIONS
- Did anyone feel intimidated during play?
- How important was your ability to see or hear?
- Were you afraid of being injured?
- Did anyone get frustrated?
- Did you notice others around you?
- Did you feel like others were watching you?

HI, LOW, YO

LEARNING EXPERIENCE
Understanding sensory impairments

EQUIPMENT
None

DESCRIPTION
The students play this game in groups of 10 to 15 in circle formation. This is a game of elimination, and once a student is eliminated he or she steps out of the circle and becomes a "heckler." The heckler's job is to walk around the outside of the circle and repeat the words "Hi," "Low," or "Yo" in an attempt to over-stimulate others that are still in the circle. They are not allowed to touch others, but they are allowed to speak louder than normal without yelling.

The game starts with one student saying "Hi" while pointing with either hand at the level of his or her forehead (as if saluting) in order to pass the turn to another player. If the student points to the right, then the student to the right says "Low" while pointing with either hand (a salute) at chin level to pass the turn to another player. If this student points to the left, then the student to the left says "Yo" and points with the whole arm to anyone in the circle to pass the turn to someone else. The sequence continues with "Hi," "Low," and "Yo" throughout the whole game. If anyone says the wrong word or points incorrectly during his or her turn, that player is eliminated and becomes a heckler who makes it difficult for others to concentrate. The players have to pay attention to the direction someone is pointing in, which could be left or right, in order to know whose turn is next. Players can pass the turn back to the person who passed to them. Eventually the game becomes a competition between two students, and finally there is one person remaining. I have never introduced this game to a group of students of any age who did not like it or who were not very distracted by the hecklers.

SAFETY ISSUES
Warn students that the hecklers will be distracting and that no one should become upset.

▶ Hi, Low, Yo.

VARIATIONS
- Play the game in larger or smaller groups.
- Practice the game with partners to help the students get used to the sequencing.

DISCUSSION QUESTIONS
- Was it difficult to concentrate with the external noise?
- How did you cope with the noise?
- Could you imagine life if you were subjected to overstimulation every day, all day long?

CHRONOLOGICAL LINE-UP

LEARNING EXPERIENCE
Understanding visual and verbal impairments; developing teamwork

EQUIPMENT AND MATERIALS
Blindfolds

DESCRIPTION
Inform the students that you are about to give them a task to complete and from this point forward they are not allowed to speak unless they need to ask you a question before the task begins. At this point have each student put on a blindfold with the exception of one student, who will be mute but sighted.

Instruct the students that they will be attempting to line up in shoe size order without speaking to anyone in the group. The student who is mute will be somewhat of a leader but of course will not be able to speak. This student will have to decide how and where to start the line, how to "discuss" the shoe sizes, and when to know that the task has been completed. All of this will occur without speaking and may be uncomfortable and somewhat frustrating for some students. Be prepared to redirect the group as the need arises.

SAFETY ISSUES
- Make sure that the area is free of obstacles and inform students when they are in close proximity to walls, bleachers, or other obstacles.
- Discuss safety issues and rules of etiquette, such as no pulling or pushing others.
- Inform the students that their balance may be affected when they lose their eyesight, and be aware that some students will be very uncomfortable using the blindfold and may need modifications of their own.

VARIATIONS
- Students line up in alphabetical order by first name or last name or by age, height, or gender.
- No sighted students. Allow one or two students to be HI as well as VI.

DISCUSSION QUESTIONS
- How did it feel to be without your sight?
- Was it frustrating not being able to speak?
- How did you communicate?
- Which do you think is more difficult, having no eyesight or no speech?
- Did your other senses overcompensate for your losses?

CENTERS FOR UNDERSTANDING

LEARNING EXPERIENCE
Understanding orthopedic and visual impairments and dyslexia

EQUIPMENT AND MATERIALS
Large-size shirts that button, gloves, tape, Velcro belts, mirrors, paper, pencils, hoops, scooters, rackets, ropes, low volleyball net, beach balls, balloons, wheelchairs, and blindfolds or goggles with tape to obscure vision

DESCRIPTION
Use learning stations to simulate disabilities and have the students choose a partner to participate with in the stations:
- Station 1: Provide gloves for the students to wear while they attempt to button a larger shirt over their own clothes and then tie their shoes; next, the students will attempt to write their names on a piece of paper while using a mirror. Students look in the mirror and not at the paper they are writing on.

- Station 2: Students pair up to practice striking skills. One student has on a glove with the thumb taped down (to provide a degree of disablement), and the partner passes balls for him or her to hit with a paddle or racket. Each partner takes a turn. Also, if possible, use Velcro straps to strap the striker's arm down for further disablement. Some students may want to practice the skills VI or blind.
- Station 3: Students participate in a game of volleyball using a shorter net. They will have varying disabilities such as blindness (blindfolds), VI (goggles), or orthopedic impairment (OI; gloves and straps) or will be in a wheelchair borrowed from the nurse's office. Allow the students to use beach balls or balloons as the volleyballs.
- Station 4: Students pull themselves on a scooter or in a wheelchair with a rope tied to the bleachers or a door. Using the props provided, the students will be blind, VI, or OI. Students may also push or pull their disabled partner on the scooter.
- Station 5: Students alternate hula hooping, jumping rope, and bowling with a partner. Again, the students will be blind or OI. While jumping rope they must work together to figure out how to turn the rope with each disability, as well as how to hula hoop. For the bowling, set up a few pins and allow the students to roll the ball to knock the pins down.

SAFETY ISSUES
- Discuss the importance of communication.
- There should be no horseplay or kidding around.

VARIATIONS
- Reorganize the stations based on specific needs.
- Use more or fewer stations based on class time limits.

DISCUSSION QUESTIONS
- How did it feel to depend on others to help you?
- Discuss some things that your partner did to assist you.
- How did your disability affect your participation?
- Discuss the importance of being patient with others who are disabled.

MOBILITY OBSTACLE COURSE

LEARNING EXPERIENCE
Understanding orthopedic and visual impairments

EQUIPMENT AND MATERIALS
Cones, over and under dowels, mats, ropes, hoops, tape, balance beam

DESCRIPTION
Design a basic obstacle course of overs and unders inside the gym. The course can be one continuous course, or it can be several courses side by side to provide the opportunity for more students to participate. Also, each student

has a partner to alternate his or her disability with to go through the course. The following is a sample course:

- Obstacle 1: Balance beam. The student with VI has to be led, and the student with OI has to be assisted. For the student in a wheelchair (or on a scooter if no chairs are available), tape a design or a line on the floor for the student to roll along.
- Obstacle 2: Use two cones and a dowel to make an obstacle for the students to crawl under. Students with VI and OI must be assisted. The student in a wheelchair needs a higher obstacle to go under.
- Obstacle 3: Tape hoops to the floor for the students to hop through. Students with VI and OI will need assistance and may need to step instead of hopping through the hoops. Students in wheelchairs may be allowed to weave through the hoops.
- Obstacle 4: Set up an obstacle of three or more stacked mats to climb over, and remember to have a mat on the ground for the students to land on. Students with OI and VI will need assistance. Provide the students in wheelchairs an under with cones and a dowel, or allow them to climb over the mats without using their legs (use Velcro straps to strap their legs together if possible to really provide the feeling of loss of the lower body). They will also need assistance, but do not allow others to lift them.
- Obstacle 5: Set up four or five cones for the students to weave through as the last obstacle. Assist students with VI or OI.

SAFETY ISSUES

- Discuss the importance of assisting others and stress that there should be no horseplay or kidding around.
- Students should not pass others on the obstacles, and all students should use a slow speed.

VARIATIONS

- Set up obstacles based on available equipment and space.
- Provide earplugs for some students, or turn the music really loud to provide overstimulation for a short while.

DISCUSSION QUESTIONS

- How important was your peer helper?
- Did you trust your peer helper? Why or why not?
- Did you enjoy being a peer helper?
- Discuss some of the ways the peers helped.
- Discuss the importance of communication.

WHEELCHAIR AND SCOOTER NOODLE VOLLEY

EXPERIENCE
Understanding limitations inherent in using a wheelchair

EQUIPMENT AND MATERIALS
Wheelchairs, scooters, noodles, and balloons or beach balls

DESCRIPTION
Set up the playing area with two parallel boundary lines for the goals. The sidelines of the basketball court are a perfect setup. Some students will be playing while sitting on the scooters and others will be playing from the wheelchairs. Team A starts on one sideline and tries to strike their balloon with the noodles in an attempt to get it over the opposite sideline (Team B's). At the same time, Team B is attempting to hit their balloon over Team A's sideline. Both teams are allowed to play offense and defense. Once a team scores, the game restarts, with both teams on their respective goal lines. Some groups even attempt to strategize. Remember that some students will be playing while sitting on the scooters and others will be playing from the wheelchairs. I have found that if I give each team a balloon, the game is less chaotic.

SAFETY ISSUES
- Warn students to be considerate of others on the scooters.
- No roughhousing.
- Players are not allowed to get off the scooters or out of the chairs to retrieve or strike the balloon.

VARIATIONS
- Allow a few students to play from a standing position. These students can play the game or assist in retrieving balloons and keeping them in the play area.

▶ Wheelchair and Scooter Noodle Volley.

- Add other disabilities to the game; for example, you can use a Velcro strap to hold down a student's arm for an OI or have a student wear earplugs or headphones to simulate HI.

DISCUSSION QUESTIONS

- Is it frustrating to have limited reach while sitting on a scooter or in a chair?
- What kind of teamwork is needed for the game?
- How important is communication?
- Did you prefer to be an offensive or a defensive player? Explain.

STATIONS FOR UNDERSTANDING

My school system and others recognize Exceptional Children's Week each year in March. The schools plan activities throughout the week in the classroom and gym to help general students understand disabilities. The following stations were used in a few of our elementary physical education classes to teach the general students empathy and to help them understand some of the challenges that our students with exceptionalities deal with each day. Students participate in each station with a partner. One student is the participant, and the partner is the assistant who monitors safety. Once the students have gone through the course, they switch positions. Safety must be discussed during the initial explanation of the stations.

STATION 1: SCOOTER PULLS (OI, VI)

Ropes are attached to the bleachers, and a scooter is provided for each rope. One partner holds the rope as the other partner pulls him- or herself toward the bleachers using only one arm. This student is asked to put one hand in a pocket to simulate impairment of the upper body. The students then alternate positions. Variation: If time permits, near the end of the session the students may also perform the activity with blindfolds.

STATION 2: LINE BALL (VI)

Set up two parallel lines about 10 to 15 feet (3 to 4.6 meters) apart. Have five or more students sit on each line wearing blindfolds. The object of the game is to strike a ball over the opponents' boundary line. The balls will have bells in them, and the students must depend on their hearing to play the game. Have the players rotate in and out of the game each 2 or 3 minutes. Sighted students can be assigned to retrieve balls when they are not playing. Set up two games if space permits.

STATION 3: OBSTACLE COURSE (VI, OI, WHEELCHAIR)

Various obstacles are set up in the middle area of the court. Each student has a partner to assist throughout the course. Some students will wear blindfolds (VI); others will put both hands in their pockets (OI); and others will use a scooter (wheelchair) to go through the course. Partners switch positions after completing the course. (For the obstacles, have students use a balance beam, go under a high hurdle, go over two low hurdles, climb over a stack of mats, step on spots, go under a higher hurdle, and weave through cones.)

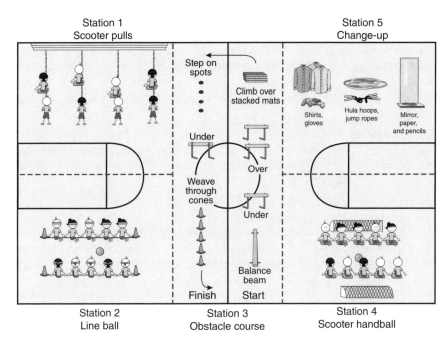

Station 1
Scooter pulls

Station 5
Change-up

Station 2
Line ball

Station 3
Obstacle course

Station 4
Scooter handball

▶ Stations for Understanding.

STATION 4: SCOOTER HANDBALL (WHEELCHAIR)
Set up two small hockey or soccer goals and have five players for each team on scooters. The teams attempt to pass the ball to team members and throw the ball into the opponents' goal. On the scooters, the players are allowed to maneuver using only their hands and arms, no legs. This will give them an idea of some of the challenges that a student in a wheelchair faces. Rotate players each 2 or 3 minutes.

STATION 5: CHANGE-UP (OI, VI, DYSLEXIA)
This station includes three activities. (1) The students wear gloves and attempt to button a large shirt over their own clothes; (2) they attempt to hula hoop and jump rope with an OI or VI; (3) they attempt to write their names on a piece of paper while looking into a mirror.

CIRCLE UP

LEARNING EXPERIENCE
Understanding VI

EQUIPMENT AND MATERIALS
Large or small bell balls, blindfolds or goggles or both

DESCRIPTION

Instruct students wearing blindfolds or goggles to sit in circles of 10 to 15. The game is very simple; the players roll the ball around in the circle, trying to keep it in play. The students will need to listen for the sound of the bells in order to track the ball. Once a player stops the rolled ball, he or she will roll the ball to another player in the circle. There is no scoring, only the opportunity to participate.

SAFETY ISSUES

Students are not allowed to throw the ball, mainly for the obvious reason that the receiver cannot see the ball coming. In addition, bell balls are not light or soft enough to be thrown at others.

VARIATIONS

- Have the roller call the name of the person he or she would like to roll the ball to, and have that person respond with a verbal cue for the ball to be rolled. Then the receiver continues the game in the same manner. This variation necessitates more communication and remaining focused.
- In conjunction, allow some students to be HI instead of or in addition to VI.

DISCUSSION QUESTIONS

- Was this game difficult for you? Explain.
- Did you enjoy playing the game without keeping score?
- Could you think of a way to keep score?

CONCLUSION

When we as teachers learn empathy for any disability, we learn to proactively and creatively include students of all abilities and exceptionalities. Eventually, we recognize that inclusion for all exceptionalities is intertwined, and then the process of inclusion becomes natural. I believe that empathy in one aspect of our lives leads to empathy in other aspects; it has a domino effect and touches others in ways that we may never understand. My hope is that you use these games for your general students and guide them toward becoming better advocates for the inclusion of all in any situation.

BIBLIOGRAPHY

Alberta Learning. (2003). Teaching students with autism spectrum disorders. http://education.alberta.ca/admin/special/resources/autism.aspx.

Bailey, R. (2001). *Teaching physical education: A handbook for primary and secondary school teachers.* New York: Routledge Falmer.

Block, M. (1994). *A teacher's guide to including students with disabilities in regular physical education.* Baltimore: Brookes.

Block, M., & Etz, K. (1995). The pocket reference: A tool for fostering inclusion. *Journal of Physical Education, Recreation and Dance, 66*(3), 47–51.

Block, M., Lieberman, L., & Conner-Kuntz, F. (1998). Authentic assessment in adapted physical education. *Journal of Physical Education, Recreation and Dance, 69*(3), 48–55.

Block, M., & Vogler, W. (1994). Inclusion in regular physical education: The research base. *Journal of Physical Education, Recreation and Dance, 65*(1), 40–42.

Boyles, N., & Contadino, D. (1998). *The learning differences sourcebook.* New York: McGraw Hill.

Centers for Disease Control and Prevention. (2004). Developmental disabilities: Cerebral palsy. www.cdc.gov/NCBDDD/dd/cp2.htm.

Conyers, M., & Wilson, D. (2005). *BrainSMART strategies for boosting test scores.* Winter Park, FL: BrainSMART.

Davis, R. (2002). *Inclusion through sports: A guide to enhancing sport experiences.* Champaign, IL: Human Kinetics.

Differentiated instruction. (2009). http://webhost.bridgew.edu/kdobush/Strategies%20for%20Teaching%20Reading/Handbook/Diff_Inst/Differentiated%20Instruction.htm.

Ervin, M. (2007). Autism spectrum disorders: Interdisciplinary teaming in schools. http://www.asha.org/about/publications/leader-online/archives/2003/q2/030415a.htm.

Gioia, G. (1993). Development and retardation. In R. Smith (Ed.), *Children with mental retardation: A parents' guide*. Bethesda, MD: Woodbine House.

Gray, C. (2000). *The new social story book: Illustrated edition*. Arlington, TX: Future Horizons.

Groft-Jones, M., & Block, M. (2006). Strategies for teaching children with autism in physical education. *Teaching Elementary Physical Education, 17*(6), 25–28.

Hensley, L. (1997). Alternative assessment for physical education. *Journal of Physical Education, Recreation and Dance, 68*(7), 19–24.

Hopper, B., Greg, J. & Maude, T. (2000). *Teaching physical education in the primary school*. New York: Routledge.

Houston-Wilson, C., & Lieberman, L. (2003). Strategies for teaching students with autism in physical education. *Journal of Physical Education, Recreation and Dance, 74*(6), 40–44.

Indiana Protection and Advocacy Services. (2008). What is IDEIA? www.in.gov/ipas/2397.htm.

Kasser, S.L. (1995). *Inclusive games*. Champaign, IL: Human Kinetics.

Krebs, L. (2005). Intellectual disabilities. In J. Winnick (Ed.) *Adapted physical education and sport*. Champaign, IL: Human Kinetics.

Landy, J.M., & Landy, M.J. (1992). *Ready-to-use P.E. activities for K-2*. Mira Loma, CA: Parker.

Lieberman, L. (Ed.). (2007). *Paraeducators in physical education: A training guide to roles and responsibilities*. Champaign, IL: Human Kinetics.

Lieberman, L., & Houston-Wilson, C. (2002). *Strategies for inclusion: A handbook for physical educators*. Champaign, IL: Human Kinetics.

Lieberman, L., James, A., & Ludwa, N. (2004). The impact of inclusion in general physical education for all students. *Journal of Physical Education, Recreation and Dance, 75*(5), 37–41.

Morris, L.R., & Schulz, L. (1989). *Creative play activities for children with disabilities*. Champaign, IL: Human Kinetics.

National Center on Physical Activity and Disability (NCPAD). (2007). *Disability/condition: Autism and considerations in recreation and physical activity settings*. www.ncpad.org/disability/fact_sheet .php?sheet = 366.

National Consortium for Physical Education and Recreation for Individuals With Disabilities. (2006). *Adapted physical education national standards*. Champaign, IL: Human Kinetics.

Pivik, J., McComas, J., & Laflamme, M. (2002). Barriers and facilitators to inclusive education. *Exceptional Children, 69*(1), 97–107.

Porretta, D. (2005). Cerebral palsy, traumatic brain injury, and stroke. In J. Winnick (Ed.), *Adapted physical education and sport.* Champaign, IL: Human Kinetics.

Richard, G. (1997). *The source for autism.* East Moline, IL: Linguisystems.

Rizzo, T., Davis, W., & Toussaint, R. (1994). Inclusion in regular classes: Breaking from traditional curricula. *Journal of Physical Education, Recreation and Dance, 65*(1), 24–26, 47.

Rouse, P. (2004). *Adapted games and activities: From tag to team building.* Champaign, IL: Human Kinetics.

Sacramento Unified School District. (2009) What is differentiated instruction? www.scusd.edu/gate_ext_learning/differentiated.htm.

Sherrill, C., Heikinaro-Johansson, P., & Slininger, D. (1994). Equal-status relationships in the gym. *Journal of Physical Education, Recreation and Dance, 65*(1), 27–31, 56.

Smith, S. (2005). Beyond games, gadgets, and gimmicks: Differentiating instruction across domains in physical education. *Journal of Physical Education, Recreation and Dance, 76*(8), 38–45.

Spungin, S. (Ed.). (2002). *When you have a visually impaired student in your classroom: A guide for teachers.* New York: AFB Press.

Stopka, C. (2006). *The teacher's survival guide: Adaptations to optimize the inclusion of students of all ages with disabilities in your program.* Blacksburg, VA: PE Central.

Tomlinson, C.A. (1999). *The differentiated classroom: Responding to the needs of all learners.* Upper Saddle River, NJ: Prentice Hall.

Tomlinson, C.A., & Allan, S.D. (2000). *Leadership for differentiating schools and classrooms.* Alexandria, VA: Association for Supervision & Curriculum Development.

U.S. Department of Education. (2006). Least restrictive environment. http://idea.ed.gov/explore/view/p/%2Croot%2Cstatute%2CI%2CB%2C612%2Ca%2C5%2C.

Wallin, J.M. (2009). An introduction to social stories. www.polyxo.com/socialstories/introduction.html.

Walsh, J. (2008). Differentiation in health and physical education. www.ophea.net/Ophea/Ophea.net/Differentiation-Health-Physical-Education.cfm.

Watson, S. (2008). What is inclusion? http://specialed.about.com/cs/integration/a/inclusion.htm.

Weber, R., & Thorpe, J. (1992). Teaching children with autism through task variation in physical education. *Exceptional Children, 59*(1), 77–86.

Widget Software. (2007). Writing with symbols 2000. [Computer software program]. Solana Beach, CA: Mayer-Johnson.

Winnick, J. (2005). *Adapted physical education and sport.* Champaign, IL: Human Kinetics.

Wolfberg, P. (1999). *Play and imagination in children with autism.* New York: Teachers College Press.

ABOUT THE AUTHOR

Pattie Rouse, EdS, is an adapted physical educator in Cherokee County Schools in Georgia, where she co-created the first adapted physical education program in the school system. She has been working with people with disabilities since 1982. In addition to her physical education teaching, she has been educating teachers and paraeducators on inclusion for many years through informal consultations as well as through staff development and professional workshops.

A co-coordinator of Special Olympics in Cherokee County, she has coached Special Olympics basketball. Throughout her career she has included students with disabilities in her programs. She is the author of *Adapted Games and Activities,* geared toward students with intellectual disabilities. In her leisure time, Ms. Rouse enjoys mountain and road biking, hiking with her dogs, and reading. Her newest means of reaching out to the community is through an adapted recreational and fitness program for elderly people in a nursing home.

You'll find other outstanding physical education resources at
www.HumanKinetics.com

In the U.S. call 1.800.747.4457
Australia 08 8372 0999
Canada. 1.800.465.7301
Europe . . . . .+44 (0) 113 255 5665
New Zealand . . . 0064 9 448 1207

HUMAN KINETICS
The Information Leader in Physical Activity
P.O. Box 5076 • Champaign, IL 61825-5076